Praise for

MW00620597

"Karen Sands is one of those rare individuals who understands that our extended longevity unlocks major opportunities. It's a time to explore new horizons, and, be it your life, work or new business startup, I can't think of a more compelling and enlightened guide than Karen. Her book abounds with inspiring, practical, and actionable advice."

~ Elizabeth Isele,
Founder and CEO, The Global Institute for Experienced Entrepreneurship,
Senior Fellow in Social Innovation, Babson College

"Peter Drucker once said, 'Feed the opportunities. Starve the problems.' There is no greater opportunity in our lifetime than the growing population of older people, who are both producers and consumers for the new Longevity Economy. Karen Sands' book is the indispensable guide to finding your way in this new land of opportunity."

~ Harry R. Moody, Ph.D.,
Creative Longevity and Wisdom Program, Fielding Graduate University

"Always ahead of her time, Karen continues to turn the business of aging on its head, a boon for women and men."

~ Nelson Broms, Ph.D.,
Social Entrepreneur Extraordinare,
Former Chairman/Holding Company, Equitable/AXA

"An important call to action! With insight and wisdom Karen brings to light the power of Ageless Boomer women. Readers will be shocked to see what the numbers truly show. Boomer women have no idea the power they have in their hands (and their wallets) right now and will for many years to come."

~ Judy Rough, CSA,
Certified Senior Advisor, Sr. Director of Strategic Alliances
Society of Certified Senior Advisors

"Karen has knocked it out of the park AGAIN.
A data-packed, awe inspiring, and valuable resource for
any business or company owner that is looking
at the future, regardless of your industry!
This is the book to read IF you don't read any other
book on aging and business marketing this year."

~ Aaron D. Murphy,
Architect , CAPS

"A definitive book. At a defining moment."

~ Elsie Maio,
Founder of Humanity, Inc/The SoulBranding^{SM} Institute

KAREN SANDS >

GRAY IS THE NEW GREEN

Rock Your Revenues in the Longevity Economy

Broad Minded Publishing, PO Box 43, Roxbury, CT 06783-0043
Cover design and interior book design by Gloria Owens, Fish Cat Design
Back cover photo by Mary Madeiras. Author profile photo by Lisa Levart / LUSH Photography

Library of Congress Control Number: 2016903174

Sands, Karen
        Library of Congress Cataloging-in-Publication Data
        ISBN: 978-0-9849260-8-4

Disclaimers

Want to use excerpts in your e-zine/newsletter, blog, or website?

OTHER TITLES
BY KAREN SANDS

An Ageless Story

Crossing the Canyon

The Greatness Challenge

Mastering Reinvention

Visionaries Have Wrinkles

Visionaries Have Wrinkles Reflections Card Deck

Visionaries Have Wrinkles Reflections Journal

A Glimpse of Tomorrow's Promise

The Ageless Way

The Ageless Way Reflections Journal

Dedications

To Mark, my husband and biggest fan,
thank you for being the timeless embodiment of
entrepreneurship at its best.

Thank you to all my readers who are visionary leaders,
conscious social entrepreneurs,
audacious world shakers & change makers-to-be:
Your Future Starts Within These Pages!
Get ready to shape the Longevity Economy and your role in it!

Gray is truly the New Green!

GRAY IS THE NEW GREEN

Table of Contents

GRAY IS THE NEW GREEN

GRATITUDES

Reading between the lines of my books will reveal the fingerprints of many people. This book is no exception. I would like to first thank my family—most of all my awesome husband, Mark, for believing in the work I'm doing and the books I'm sharing with you.

I am also grateful to the remarkable women and men whose shoulders I stand on, and whose pioneering work shaped my thinking about business, visionary leadership and the future. These great visionaries and change makers encouraged me to sound the clarion call to those who follow in my footsteps in the sands of time. There are too many to name here, but a few I am compelled to thank: Nelson Broms, "social entrepreneur extraordinaire," who honed me into the global thinker, strategist, and futurist I've become; Ruth S. Bloch who showed me the feminine way of leadership in a man's world; Mack Hanan who encouraged me to make customer-centric marketing and sales a cornerstone of my business thinking; Dr. W. Edwards Deming, P.h.D., who catapulted my thinking to a whole new level anchored in continuous quality improvement; Peter Drucker who influenced my nascent management approach; Peter Senge and Marshall Thurber, who both introduced me to visionary leadership; Michael Port who confirmed my entrepreneurial vision for the future; Alvin Toffler who is one of my earliest futurist-heroes. To all of these truly greats, I thank you!

I worked with many gifted professionals along the way to bring *Gray is the New Green* into your hands. My deep gratitude goes to graphic artist Gloria Owens of Fish Cat

Design for the another stunning cover and book page design; to Gretchen Tipps for her invaluable expertise and guidance when this manuscript was in its last drafts, and for her final reviews as the manuscript became a book. ❯

FOREWORD BY LORI BITTER

Companies who ignore older consumers,
their ideas and their money do so at their peril.
~ Lori Bitter

Advertising and marketing principles were practically birthed with the Baby Boom generation. While the principles of storytelling to create demand and move products through the sales cycle has not changed, the way those messages are delivered has been impacted in ways we never could have foreseen. And we have all adapted to the highly targeted world of digital communications.

Yet our ability to "follow the money" and understand how to look for lucrative consumer segments is "stuck." It is easy to understand how. Much of what we know about modern marketing is based on the Mad Men era of the late 50's and early 60's – that post war period of relative prosperity. The most important artifact of this period was birth of the first real consumer market of young people—the result of the baby boom.

Rather than going from childhood to work or war, young people grew into a new life stage – teenager and then young adult – and were afforded access to education. Where we lived, what we drove, the music we listened to and how we dressed all changed. Gender roles were bent. The world came into our living rooms through the power of television. Our love affair with youth was in full blossom.

Like any affair, who we fell in love with was not who we married. We fawned over the optimism and hope of this period, but we stuck the label of "youth" on it and have been dragging that ball and chain around for decades – when simple demographic analysis and cues in popular culture were telling us otherwise.

Karen Sands sets us free in *Gray is the New Green* by showing us how the Baby Boom generation is embracing maturity in an Ageless way and leading the consumer marketplace, as well as the new world of work. It is a story of how women have grown to be the powerhouse consumers in nearly every product category, none more so than the women of the boom. It is also about the evolution of hope and optimism.

And in a time when Sally Field and Robert DeNiro are still starring in movies, young people are dying their hair grey to be "on fleek", and a 61 year old model is rocking the pages of *Sports Illustrated's Swimsuit Edition*, Karen deftly points out that many industries still can not or will not read the tea leaves. Older consumers are either left out of the conversation, or are not spoken to in the language of Agelessness. For that, companies leave money on the table.

Karen takes us on a carefully woven journey through the signposts of change as we seize both the challenges and opportunities of our increased longevity. From the rise of female power in both the marketplace and the workplace, to the idea of an "un-retirement" for money, passion or both, this generation of older adults is rebranding the idea of old age – without the benefit of any ad agency.

Now the generation that created the stage of young adulthood is defining and leading this new stage of life by being what they have always been - intellectually curious, optimistic and driven. The lesson in *Gray is the New Green* is that companies who ignore older consumers, their ideas and their money do so at their peril. In many ways "gray power" is emerging as powerfully as the women's movement did in the 1960s. Baby boomers have no capacity for quietly riding into the sunset.

The statistics Karen shares are compelling. As the saying goes, facts illustrate, but stories illuminate. The value of this book is in the stories of how we got here and who will lead us to a new world of multi-generation living, working and thinking. The *Reflections* at the close of each chapter are a bonus that makes this book a valuable planning tool, in addition to a great read.

You can trust Karen's experience as the leading GeroFuturist to guide you to the green in these trends, and expand your thinking about the potential of the graying market.

Read on and join the movement!

Lori Bitter

Author, *The Grandparent Economy – How Baby Boomers Are Bridging the Generation Gap*

CEO, The Business of Aging

ABOUT REFLECTIONS QUESTIONS

Questions at the end of each chapter to help you find your distinct path to rocking your revenues in the Longevity Economy.

Each new story or phase of life needs a creative approach to move beyond the past into a creative new hope-filled future story with the new tasks that it encompasses.

I'd like to shine a light to guide you on your quest to *The Ageless Way* by including some suggestions for getting the most out of this book. Consider my suggestions as a guide.

I've included *Reflections* at the end of each chapter to translate the substance of each chapter into portable tools for your own illumination. These *Reflections* are intended as jumping-off points for you to dig in to the chapter material as deep as you desire. I have arranged these in the general order as they arise by chapter.

Putting something in writing often solidifies new material in our minds, and allows new "ahas" to arise unimpeded. Consider writing down your answers to the *Reflections* provided at the end of each chapter instead of just scanning or reading them and moving on.

My suggestion is that you familiarize yourself with these reflective questions and exercises by doing them once through in the order they appear. However, once you've read through the book, or a particular chapter, I encourage you to use them in any sequence that suits you.

What works well is to make a copy of the *Reflections* and then spend focused time reflecting and writing down your answers. Commit to returning to these questions regularly to see how your answers change over time.

When you are ready to give your focused time to a chapter's *Reflections*, find a quiet space for reflection at a time when you won't be disturbed. You may want to settle into your favorite comfy chair or another spot that is your special chilling out, meditating, or time-out reflecting place. Relax using any process that has worked for you in the past, perhaps using a series of deep breaths and slowly relaxing and letting go wherever there is tension in your body. You'll know when you are ready to gently come back into the room. Be sure you have a pen and the list of *Reflections* you will be working on close at hand. Give yourself at least fifteen to twenty minutes at each sitting to journal your responses and insights gained. I have found that these *Reflections* will provide invaluable insights if you give yourself the gift of reserved, uninterrupted time to be with yourself.

If you have any questions or you want to share your "ahas" or stories, please send them to me directly at Karen@KarenSands.com, putting "GNG queries" in the subject line.

Thank you for joining me on the quest to *The Ageless Way.*

– Karen

Chapter 1

GRAY IS THE NEW GREEN

*The problem is that as people have matured and markets have evolved, marketing has not.
...Clearly marketers have to change a great deal to adjust to this new world order.*

~ David Wolfe

Without a doubt, the most massive transformation we're undergoing as a nation (and around the globe) is catalyzed by the "change-every-thing-in-its-path" Gray Force Field of Baby Boomers (born 1943*-1964), approaching or past traditional retirement age. Boomers control more than 75 percent of our nation's wealth, and

---

* Never hold Boomers to fixed definitions. We have a propensity to self-contradict and change the rules as we evolve (e.g., "Don't trust anyone over thirty!"). So don't waste your time constraining us by rigid cohort groups. A wide spectrum of opinions exist on what *is* a Baby Boomer, demographically, historically, and culturally. The U.S. Census Bureau brackets Boomers based on the spike (boom) in birthrate from 1946 to 1964. Perhaps because this is an easy range to recall, it has garnered widespread popularity. However, I find myself in the camp embracing 1943 as the starting year of the Baby Boomer generation. I'm in good company with Landon Jones, in his book *Great Expectations: America & the Baby Boom Generation* (1980). Authors William Strauss and Neil Howe, creators of the Strauss-Howe generational theory, also define the social generation of Boomers inclusive of those born starting in 1943. No matter which generation we are referring to it is important to soften the boundaries of our definitions so that we are inclusive of less defined beginnings and endings to allow for the gray areas.

they are spending that wealth, outpacing other generations in nearly every buying category. Even if Boomers work less, we're still talking about a starting point of $2.4 trillion in annual income. Combine this with the fact that women alone control 85 percent of consumer spending, and that they outlive men by about five or six years (according to Scientific American, there are six women to every four men by age 85), and the conclusion is clear: Women mean business.

But that's not all. Boomer Women mean BIG BUSINESS. Just look at these statistics:

- United States women over 50 control $19 trillion.
- Women over 50 control more than three-quarters of U.S. financial wealth.
- People over 50 are 43 percent of U.S. adults and 27 percent of the total U.S. population.
- Women age 50-plus are 23.7 percent of U.S. adults.
- Seventy-five million-plus U.S. women over the age of 50 are working outside the home.
- Between 1997 and 2013, the number of U.S. woman-owned businesses grew by 59 percent, vs. 41 percent for all new businesses in the United States; a rate almost one and a half times the average.

Ageless Women are where it's at!

Everyone from solopreneurs to large corporations needs to recognize that this market is essential to staying in business in the future, or even in the present. Especially important is that Ageless Women themselves are in a unique position to serve this market just as they are in this market to be served. In other words, gray is the new green!

As author David Wolfe observed, "I believe companies are largely ignoring the largest and richest customer group in history for three reasons. First, stereotypical beliefs about older customers paint them as resistant to change, so why bother. Second, there is widespread uneasiness about how to market to older customers, so let's spare ourselves the pain of failure. Third, people under 40, who are not in the same mental space as members of the new adult marketplace majority, dominate marketing processes. They relate most comfortably to customers of their own ages or younger."

Yet, the economy, business, and the workplace are all undergoing glacial change from the status quo, despite a combination of massive upheavals and a constant media focus on the aging Boomer population. Throughout history, chaos and major shifts have always been accompanied by renewed attempts to hold on for dear life to the (false) security of How Things Have Always Been Done. There is an ongoing conflict between the stories of our past and the stories of our future, and the battlefield between them is inevitably our present story.

The Truth about Our Future

Knowing full well that the maturing Boomer generation was about to turn aging on its head, in the late 1980s I set out to sound the clarion call of gray is the new green. For years wherever I showed up I provocatively asked, "Are you leaving money on the table by ignoring the Baby Boomer boom?" I continue to ask this question today.

My message continues to be, "Here's how to stay in sync with the generation that keeps you in business." I present to

professional and corporate marketers, strategists, and entrepreneurs (experienced and newbies) across many sectors. I
attempt to wake up those who have the most to gain or lose in
market share and reach if they close their eyes to the 40-plus
market potential. I warn them that they best get on board
fast, because their ability to monetize going forward will be
based on their willingness to serve this enormous force field of
new Boomer demand in the workplace, the U.S. marketplace,
and around the globe.

I continue to travel the country to present one of my
signature talks, "Visionaries Have Wrinkles: Serving the
Generation Who Will Change the World…Again" to my fellow
futurists, academicians, coaches, consultants, gerontologists,
and all manner of professionals from marketers and service-
providers to product companies, those in financial services,
and from large to small businesses, including solopreneurs.

A small percentage of marketers "get" what is coming, so
they are leaping ahead to own segments of this market. Others,
studies reveal, may be undervaluing a key demographic and
losing a changing game.

Most businesses are still trying to figure out what Baby
Boomers want, and Boomers are still trying to figure out what
they want. The Gray Tsunami is heading to Madison Avenue
and Main Street, USA.

No matter your industry or field, those who recognize
the new rules of the game will reap the benefits and gobble
up market share. For starters, the new rules are customer-
centric, not product-centered, as has been the case for eons.
At least until Millennials turn 40, youth no longer rules! But
"PrimeTime Women" do! More on this later in this chapter.

Let's get back to the here and now stats that should blow your socks off! Based on a briefing paper prepared by Oxford Economics for AARP, it is estimated that "a 106 million-plus market is expected to grow by over 30% in the next 20 years." If you snooze, you lose. Any entrepreneur or service professional who ignores the enormous power of the Big Gray already on our threshold might as well kiss her business goodbye. To anyone not paying attention, I must ask, are you sure you want to leave money on the table by ignoring this 40-plus market?

If you are not already serving or planning to serve the 40-plus market, you are not only missing out financially—you are missing out on the chance to align what matters with an audience that is consciously choosing companies that are making a difference as well as a profit.

The aftermath of the Great Recession can seem like the worst possible time to focus your business on your values, but the opposite is true. Boomers are an indication of how your clients are changing. Living your values and focusing on what matters in your business is not only what you need; it's what the world needs—and it's what the world is willing to pay for.

Businesses that want to tap into this trend must shift their focus from value to values, from the bottom line to the Triple Bottom Line: People, Planet, Profit.

Just consider how this trend is likely to play out. People and businesses that find a way to combine a larger visionary purpose with their business model will be the most profitable. More people and businesses will follow their lead until visionary business practices become the norm. Not riding this trend now not only means missing out on a larger market, more money, and greater impact—it could make your ideas and your business ultimately obsolete.

Boomer women over 50 grew up watching prime-time TV and now are emerging as the hottest market to serve. Some of us, like myself, fall into the "Boomer Classic" grouping of those who were born and grew up in the 1940s and 1950s. The oldest Boomers, referred to as Leading Edge Boomers, are heading into their seventies. The next wave, the Later Edge Boomers, were born and grew up in the 1960s and 1970s.

There's a lot of talk in marketing and advertising circles these days about splitting up these two groupings. Why is this distinction between Leading Edge Boomers vs. later-born Boomers important to know?

In some important ways these two groupings are vastly different based on their formative adolescent experiences. I learned this early on when my then-graphics designer, a classic Leading Edge Boomer, when reviewing my website plans declared, "I don't like being lumped in with my younger Boomer sisters. I love them, but they were not 'sistas.' I was a flower child, I wanted to save and change the world. I was/am about peace, love and rock 'n' roll. My sisters were the "Me" generation, all about getting more, not into the world around them. We are no way the same generation!"

I'm all for inclusivity, but it's important in crafting our marketing and branding messages to recognize the disparity between Leading Edge Boomers and their younger Boomer counterparts, labeled as Later Edge Boomers (aka, the Me Generation, Generation Jones, and Trailing-Edge Boomers). What is critical to glean is that all Baby Boomers have suffered and come through a tragic reversal of our youthful idealized "we-can-all-have-it-all" Boomer story. We went from "life is good" to tragedies within each decade to now having the dream's downfall be additionally triggered by unforeseen events outside our control (like natural disasters, the long Great Recession, a world taken over by extremists—terrorism, cyber crime) and our Mother Earth fighting for the planet's life as we know it. We now need to re-story the Boomer story.

Leading-Edge women Baby Boomers (born between 1943 and 1955) moved through adolescence and into adulthood in a drastically different time of chaos and tragedy that scarred our youthful aspirations for the future. Seventy-eight days after the assassination of JFK, the Beatles arrived on the American scene. Then we lost Martin Luther King Jr. We were in deep mourning, but we grew up with rock 'n' roll. We came of age during the Vietnam War era and experienced the draft. We grew up in a time of cultural rule changing and intense social upheaval. Dylan and the Beatles gave us hope, stoked our revolutionary dreams again. We had transistor radios back then. Remember them? What about black-and-white TVs? I couldn't wait to see the next episode of *Zorro, Bat Masterson* and most memorable of all, *The Twilight Zone*. I can still hear Rod Sterling guiding us behind the outer curtain of time and space into another plane of existence. Scary and addicting. My folks loved Ed Sullivan, and we all loved *I Love Lucy* and *The Honeymooners*. My younger sister was the epitome of Boomer youth. She was into political unrest, anti-war protests and riots, social experimentation, sexual freedom, drug experimentation, and everything associated with the Woodstock culture. We all shared the awe of the first moon walk and the Civil Rights and the Second Wave Feminist movements of the 1970s.

The Later Edge Boomers (born between 1956 and 1964) bypassed much of that Leading-Edge rocky youth. Per a good description of Boomers on Wikipedia, their defining experiences were "the Cold War, Vietnam War, Watergate and Nixon's resignation, lowered drinking age in many states 1970-1976, the oil embargo, raging inflation, gasoline shortages, Jimmy Carter's imposition of registration for the draft, Ronald Reagan and Live Aid." Their music was a blend of rock, pop, disco, some punk and funk. My sister loved watching *The Brady Bunch* and *Happy Days*. Birth control was taken for granted, as were graduate school and plentiful career opportunities.

Caveat to share. Women born in the mid-1950s found themselves in the midst of these two coming-of-age cohort groups (seemingly polar opposites on the generational range and spectrum). Are you one of these women? I bet you also remember where you were when JFK was assassinated. Did you play the Beatles at recess and listen to Dylan on the radio? Even though you were too young to participate fully, these events and people were formative for you, too.

Wikipedia goes on to list the key characteristics of Leading-Edge Baby Boomers as experimental, individualists, free-spirited, and social cause oriented. On the other hand, these are the characteristics listed for the Later-Edge Boomers: less optimistic, distrustful of government, and generally cynical. Again descriptive of extremes. Back to extreme characterization and categorization. Mixed in are those who find themselves psychologically and behaviorally profiled in the wrong end of the generation. Remember, these are generalized descriptive profiles based on data profiling. If I missed you in my attempt to share some defining distinctions within the enormous Baby Boomer generation, please let me know by email so that we together can keep redefining to be inclusive. (Please send to Karen@KarenSands.com and put "GNG" in the subject line.)

Now all of our assumptions about how the world works were in disarray. But it wasn't supposed to be this way—even for the "one percent!" Now the whole range of Baby Boomers have incomplete, or unfinished stories. We've moved from burning with passion for change, to burning up with impotent rage and then being burned out. Many Boomers who once thought being a Boomer was awesome now think the 1960s failed. Many of us have broken hearts and weary Souls after realizing that the tragic reversal that befell us is so much bigger than we are. We thought we'd be coasting right about now. Instead, we have been in shock and awe in the face of the enormity of devastating loss all around us. People have lost their savings. Planned pensions have evaporated. Our homes have been taken from us or we have lost our equity. Rampant but hard-to-diagnose PTSD plagues us after learning we really are not completely in charge of our story. OMG, we are not masters of our selves after all. What a cosmic death has been visited on Baby Boomers who were pioneers in self-actualization and intent on a cosmic connection. We lost our *whole* Boomer story; we are still in a survival mode with uncertainly our constant shadow. What a mess!

In David Wolfe's 2003 book, *Ageless Marketing,* he writes of the fall out from our Boomer tumble from grace: "Uncertainty reigns, but this much is certain: To regain a steady hand on the directions of our work, our society, and perhaps our own lives, we must unlearn a host of old rules and learn many new ones. There is no more daunting task we face than to adapt to the idea that much of what we thought we knew is wrong." But isn't older age all about living in grace, being transcendent, and winding down to the good life? Post our tragic fall, we now seek warmth around the campfire flames, rather than the ravaging rage and hopeless despair that has been ever present during the Great Recession of the twenty-first century and into the years following.

Turns out everything before now was just a dress rehearsal. We've lived through tragic reversal of fortunes to learn what really, truly matters. This is the same for both ends of the Boomer demographic. We are still re-evaluating, reimagining, reintegrating, and going through values-based reinvention. What carries us forward is that we are re-storying and reclaiming our tomorrows based on our values and what matters most.

There are a couple more wrinkles in the Boomer women's story. We've had two cognitive jolts that change everything for us going forward! We've never had this many women living healthy and long lives, nor have we experienced post-menopausal brain before, much less in these numbers.

I have long called the symptomatic changes that come with "The Change" a "Trick of the Feminine." Perimeno-pausal symptoms like brain fog, hot flashes, mood swings, and vibrant dreamtime force us to "pause" so we can go deeper into examining our lives to date, reclaiming parts of ourselves long ago left behind and tossing those that no longer work for us. These biochemical hormonal shifts foster deep cellular and psychic openings that form new pathways to access our deeper truths and embrace the wild, wise energy of the archetypal Inner Crone.

No small wonder that this menopausal-induced shift into our inner psyche coincides with a tendency to create a renewed orientation to our right brain as our primary orientation, with our left brain moving into a support function. This inward shift brings with it an increased ability to access both our metaphorical right brain processing and intuitive feminine knowing. No wonder Jungians have long referred to the right-brain processing function being associated with the inner feminine, our psyche, our Soul, whereas the left-brain analytical, goal-focused processing function is associated with the inner masculine, our mind, our spirit.

Considering that the average age of the onset of menopause is 51, I am always in wonderment that "The Change" occurs as we women developmentally and chronologically move into the midpoint of our midlife course.

For three hundred years or so, women were kept as bare-foot girls and then impregnated young women with short life spans. Now, with elongating lifespans and the advent of new findings in neuroscience, women are just beginning to discover and tap into potent post-menopausal brains in numbers never known before. In my view, this rising of women and the inner feminine (divine and sacred dark) happening is not coincidental; it is synchronistic, which leads me to believe that we older women will bring new intuitive foresight and imagination, and a vast number of new possibilities, to the forefront. We can radically reframe the stories we tell ourselves about aging, as well as confront modern-day global issues like hunger, climate change, barbaric terrorism, deadly plagues, rising misogyny, oppression, and more.

Post-40 women will become the source and resource of most of the new evolutionary visionary thinking and whole-brain wisdom leadership skills for our re-storied times. This will neither replace nor displace the inner masculine, nor the men in our lives. Rather, we will partner with our menfolk to usher in a new Feminine era where what matters most, for everyone, drives our future.

Now, as we enter our middle and later years, we are retrieving interrupted and unfinished stories to reshape our new story endings. We are returning to our first and earlier chapters to rewrite a new Aspirational Ageless Future, while creating new legacies that matter far into future generations.

Word to the Wise

What worked in the past to garner our Boomer women's attention and gain loyalty won't work today. We don't have time to waste, so skip the B.S. Only straight-up transparency and authentic outreach will make a dent. The only way through to our pocketbooks is story telling based on our core values and valuing our personal stories as meaningful.

Businesses that target boomers will need to ask deeper questions. ...Businesses that understand dream fulfillment, lifestage marketing, and the desire of baby boomers to make a difference will lead the pack.

~ Mary Furlong, *Turning Silver into Gold*

Too Big to Fail

I can attest to those stories about "too big to fail" companies that are so mired in *what was* and *what worked* in the past that they totally miss the opportunity that is coming down the pike…it's already here.

My all-time favorite women business writer, Harvard Professor Rosabeth Moss Kanter, described and categorized these same behemoths in her 1990 book, *When Giants Learn to Dance.* I was still considered a "new breed" intrapreneur in the financial services industry when I first read Kanter's book in which she disrobes the dysfunctional nature of financial services in particular. Kanter's astute commentary still applies to all forms of business entities and institutions, especially when it comes to the lack of foresight and the next-to-nil fleet-footed adaptation skills required to best serve this Ageless Women demographic. The financial services industry today is still mired in outmoded ways of doing business (e.g., applying dated product-driven and transaction-centered approaches vs. providing a customer-centric relational approach, which is spot-on for this demographic).

The Hudson Institute, a prestigious think tank in Washington, D.C., describes future prospects and significant workforce changes projected over the next several decades in both of its highly respected comprehensive reports; Workforce 2000 and Workforce 2020. A key takeaway from both reports is that this unprecedented "PrimeTime" demographic shift will rear its head in the world soon, if it hasn't already. This disruptive shift will be a game changer no matter how it first emerges on your workforce radar. Some telltale signs are already showing up: your firm's dwindling number of Boomer knowledge workers, gaps in workforce skills, or the stagnation of many of your current pre-retirees who are choosing not to make waves. It may be seen in the increasing number of women leaving after working their tails off for years only to be treated as invisible after 40, or beyond their expiry date after 50. However this shift manifests, a shake-up is under way. Are you prepared or asleep at the helm?

When Baby Boomers Say Sayonara

Don't minimize a sudden exodus of Baby Boomers by thinking this mass departure will solely impact consumer products. Instead, consider its impact on every field and industry, as all will be affected. I was in total shock a few years ago when I heard from top scientists and management leadership futurist colleagues of mine in the National Aeronautics and Space Administration (aka NASA) that the majority of the agency's scientists, astronauts, and leadership are over age 50. After years of passionate dedication to the mission of NASA, due to cutbacks imposed on them, these professionals have been deflated and demoralized. In response, most are taking early retirement (or at least considering it), saying that they are done, "over and out," because they were too old for such shenanigans. This mass departure will bring with it a great loss to NASA, and to the world, given that their hard-earned knowledge goes right out the door with them.

An article in Networkworld.com woke me up by highlighting another sector implosion caused by departing Boomer knowledge workers, which is about to happen across all industries with an in-house IT organization or dedicated contracted IT department. Are you counting on Boomers to put off retiring and stick around? Counting on Baby Boomers to "hang in there" is bad planning when it comes to your IT workforce development and succession initiatives. Just ponder this for a moment. Think what would happen if all the Boomers on your team decide to leave at the same time. Wouldn't it be better to limit your exposure to brain drain directly caused by your knowledge workers retiring or changing employers?

It's important to raise the veils of denial around the conflicting stories we are told about our aging workforce and the places in which we work. A shocking, but important, denial eradicator is a study by KPMG based in the Netherlands (it is one of the largest professional service companies in the world and one of the Big Four auditors), wherein executives and HR directors were surveyed about their attitudes regarding managing older staff. When asked if there is a "silent tipping point" at which employees are "perceived to be less valuable or attractive to the organization," two-thirds of HR chiefs said there was an "over-the-hill tipping point." Almost one-half of HR directors said this tipping point occurs at 50 years old and more than one-third said at age 60. So there it is. Over the Hill is universally age 50! However, without a doubt, Baby Boomers at the helm of companies, government, and institutions across all sectors, are pushing the benchmark further along the age continuum. Whatever the moving target age is today for a pink slip, the silver ceiling is hovering over all our heads. Leading-Edge Gen Xers are moving closer and closer to the current expiry date. Does this mean Over the Hill will move to age 60 by the time Gen Xers head into their sixties?

Women in droves are bypassing not only the glass ceiling, but now the silvered glass ceiling as well. Our impact doesn't stop in the workplace. Instead, we are making change happen faster and faster…like a fast-engulfing wildfire—right into retail dressing rooms, online shopping, cosmetic counters, who and what we watch on the silver screen, and most of all, in all our coffers and spreadsheets!

Yet, giant corporations, like elephants, don't know how to dance. In fact, most of these giants, as well as the "little guys," are leaving trillions on the table, as they turn a blind eye to what's going to rock their boat…maybe even sink it.

Times They Are a-Changing

A new story is emerging, written by those marketers and product makers who recognize that it is worthwhile to get beyond the rampant malevolent ageism in corporate marketing and product development decision making. A finding in a Nielsen study projects that by 2017 Baby Boomers will control 70 percent of the country's disposable income. No surprise that only the most nimble entrepreneurs and avant-garde among us are taking the lead. The "good old boys" at the helm of the big elephant behemoths will pay the price of sticking solely with the youth market. Clearly they still haven't learned to dance decades after Kanter's call to action.

Mary Furlong, whom I refer to as the "grand dame" of the business of aging, has for decades been sounding the clarion call bringing business leaders, innovators, and investors together to capitalize on new business and investment opportunities in the longevity marketplace.

From the start in 2007, when I first read her book *Turning Silver into Gold,* and later when I learned about her annual winter What's Next Boomer Business Summit and then attended as a luncheon author-blogger table host, it was clear that there are many parallels in our respective visions for entrepreneurs in the business of aging and for the global community of women 40+. But that's not all she's up to. Furlong also offers her annual summer event, the Silicon Valley Boomer Venture Summit for entrepreneurial talent and investors. On top of all her accomplishments, Furlong is also the dean's executive professor of entrepreneurship at the Leavey School of Business at Santa Clara University and founder of SeniorNet (1986), Third Age Media (1996), and her current incarnation, Mary Furlong and Associates (2002).

Bottom line: I am inspired by Furlong because she both epitomizes an Ageless woman, and represents a true Visionary with Wrinkles. In her current leadership role at the helm of Mary Furlong and Associates (MFA), she continues to elevate the business of aging and foster innovation and entrepreneurship. You can find out more at www.maryfurlong.com.

I'd be remiss to not mention Lori Bitter, one of the new breed of women visionary leaders in the business of aging. Formerly she was president of J. Walter Thompson's Boomer division, JWT BOOM, and led client services for Age Wave Impact. Recently named to Entrepreneur magazine's 100 to Watch List, Bitter provides strategic consulting, research, and product development for companies seeking to engage with mature consumers at The Business of Aging. She also serves as publisher of GRAND—the digital magazine for grandparents. Her book, *The Grandparent Economy* (2015), is a must-read.

The Silver Screen Leads the Way

In the past, there have been fewer roles available for women over 45, except for a smattering of niche films. Word has it that Hollywood studios value men's work over women's, most definitely as they age. Older women are breaking the silver screen's once-impregnable silver ceiling with 80 percent of 2014's female Oscar nominees older than 50, including many of our favorite stars like Judi Dench (then 79) in *Philomena*, Meryl Streep (then 64) in *August: Osage County*, Emma Thompson (then 55) in *Saving Mr. Banks*, Sandra Bullock (then 50) in *Gravity*, and June Squibb (then 84) in *Nebraska*. In response to winning her first Oscar in her role as Jasmine in *Blue Jasmine* (after six previous Oscar nominations), Cate Blanchett (then 39) stated in her acceptance speech that "women's movies are no longer niche movies. Older women have powered their way into the mainstream, dominating cinemas' screens, winning awards, garnering box-office receipts, and showing the Millennials how it's done: Combine a triple threat of wisdom, talent, and patience to hone your craft."

Another new blockbuster film, *Elsa & Fred,* is appearing on the silver screen, demonstrating Hollywood's current shift in focus from producing films solely for the youth market to now offering films by and for the mature majority market. This thrills me to no end. The grand dame of America's cinema, Shirley MacLaine (80 and counting), has returned to center stage as the character Elsa. Bravo both to MacLaine and to the director, Michael Radford, who uses MacLaine's character to explore the polarities of a woman's ownership of her real chronological age vs. how she feels inwardly. This is truth-telling onscreen, which I've always admired in all of MacLaine's performances. Now MacLaine will shake us up and portray what research already bears out, that for most of us we still "see" ourselves at around age 40 whether we are in our sixties, our seventies and beyond.

For me, Kim Cattrall, who played Samantha on *Sex and the City,* tells it like it is now that she is newly turned on to finding a forum to speak to the Baby Boomer generation. Why is she so turned on? She says, "Because I feel that we are the biggest generation out there, and nobody (except PBS) is really addressing us as far as entertainment." She adds, "I want to speak about this generation in my work. I am interested in making programming for actresses and stories of women in their sixties. I'm just shocked that there isn't more programming for us out there. The biggest generation that ever was is completely ignored and I want to do something about that." Kim, if you are reading this book, please know that I'm here ready and raring to go, so give me a call anytime!

Forward-Leaning Fashion and Beauty Product Companies at the Head of the Runway

Ageism in advertising is also becoming old hat! New research shows women over the age of 50 are the highest increasing-spending demographic when it comes to fashion and beauty. Spending on clothes and accessories is increasing in the over-50 market and falling in the under-50 market.

UK's High Street fashion retailers are mirroring a quiet but fast expanding evolution in which the 50-plus women that High Street abandoned years ago are now being wooed and reclaimed for good reason: This demographic group is accounting for 41 percent of retail sales, along with an impressive 90 percent of the UK's retailers experiencing their fastest growth from this same age group. Confirming that this trend is here to stay, University of Kent's Professor Julia Twigg, author of *Fashion and Age*, says, "Women over 75 are now shopping as frequently as those in their teens and twenties were in the Sixties." Twigg goes on to say, "Now, the lives of those in their sixties are not immensely different from those in their forties." In fact, "The over-fifties are not a funny little niche to be pandered to, but a market every bit as stylish, active and alert as their daughters—and with more disposable income."

Other smart American marketers and product makers are following suit by paying attention to a Boombox survey in which almost 60 percent of Boomer women responded that they can't relate to most beauty ads and 80 percent shared that they don't aspire to look like models in those ads. Women aren't holding back any punches when they tell Boombox the real core truth: "We'd like to see more 'real people' and more 'people of our age.'" American Apparel and Marc Jacobs, both major fashion labels, as well as NARS, a cutting-edge beauty products company, and L'Oreal are jumping on the Ageless Beauty bandwagon. Breaking the age barrier, Marc Jacobs has hired 65-year-old actress Jessica Lange as the face of its new beauty campaign, NARS has chosen 68-year-old actress Charlotte Rampling as its lead, and L'Oreal has a Boomer favorite, Diane Keaton (69) as its new celebrity portrayal of *real* beauty. But that's not all. At age 69, Oscar winner Helen Mirren is the newest addition to L'Oreal's roster of stars, taking a natural approach to aging and portraying Ageless Beauty. In her own words, Mirren says, "I hope I can inspire other women towards greater confidence by making the most of their natural good looks. We are all worth it!" 63-year-old, newly found model, Jacky O'Shaughnessy, has been chosen as American Apparel's newest lingerie model instead of its usual 20-something model, proving with its new tagline that "sexy has no expiration date." All marketers and product companies can follow suit by morphing into an age-friendly, Ageless Beauty model that will both sustain their brands' leadership in the anti-aging women's market and expand market opportunities in the multi-generational legacy market as they reach across generations to mothers, daughters, and granddaughters, as well as sisters, aunts, and nieces.

Over-the-Top Ageism in Marketing and Advertising

Baby Boomer women represent the first generation in history to take full charge of their lives…at every stage.

~ Marti Barletta

Marti Barletta aptly coined Baby Boomers and Matures "PrimeTime Women." We grew up watching more television than younger viewers today. Yet a large number of older women tune out ads. I know I do. According to findings by GlynnDevins Advertising, older adults surveyed do not believe ads portray them as "people to be respected." That response should come as no surprise when scanning current advertising spots that either portray the post-50 demographic as moronic and past tense, or out of commission due to a variety of age-related "dysfunctions." Not exactly a positive depiction of older adults.

According to a Nielsen study on the state of advertising buys and the dollars spent on the post-50 market, it appears that media buyers and marketers have turned a blind eye to the over-50 demographic. The majority of media buyers and marketers consider post-50 adults worthy of only five percent or less of their advertising and marketing dollars.

The measly five percent allocated and the out-of-touch-with-reality cut-off age of 49 is no surprise, really. Advertising and marketing companies, consultancies, and internal departments are notorious for being youth-driven not only in their campaigns, but also in their hiring, promotion, and retention practices, with employee value decreasing as employees move into their mid-thirties. The Bureau of Labor Statistics (BLS) states that the median age of advertising employees is 39.3; that's approximately three years younger than all workers they studied.

But what really hurts are the ad campaigns that make us want to rage and stop buying the products associated with the in-bad-taste, over-the-top, blatant ageism. I am appalled by the recent spate of Esurance ads in which older women are depicted as old bags and dumber than dumb. The reverse mortgage ads with Fred Thompson, the former senator from Tennessee, bring instant credibility (and incredulity!) while he speaks about the benefits of his sponsor's product. What I find so distasteful is that while Thompson continues to espouse the benefits to us, the camera pans to a couple who are not using their house value to cover their lifestyle as they age, looking harried and sad as they paint their peeling white picket fence. Then, from this downer depiction, the camera pans to a different smiling, chipper, relaxed couple surrounded by their bright-colored flower garden. Give me a break. We may be over 50, or 90, but we aren't stupid. This portrayal is insulting, almost as much as the Esurance ads! The worst offenders these days are the misogynist and ageist ads by Geico and VW. Both have ads putting down older women and mothers! depicting us as ding-bats, losers or raucous self-centered older women.

Then there are the Sandals escape luxury vacation ads that speak volumes about whom they are trying to reach. What about Viagra and Cialis? For the longest time, we've been besieged in the Cialis ads by a man and woman ending up in separate four-footed tubs placed on a beach. I don't think I can easily get in and out of one of those tubs, much less look sexy doing so. Have you ever noticed that the model couples look like they shouldn't be having erectile dysfunction issues, since they all look younger than their early fifties? The newest spot now goes right to clean porn with a lovely blonde Aussie or English woman dressed in a Marilyn Monroe–like sensual beach-dress, lying down with a beguiling deep-throated plea that you men just must get over your erectile dysfunction, and when you do, look what will happen for you! Voilà! She's all yours, fellas! Okay, fan the guys' egos, get them aroused, but promises, promises.

Financial Services Still Can't Find Their Dancing Shoes

Last but not least are my long-ago colleagues in financial services who are still trailing the marketplace when it comes to women, most definitely Boomer women. From what I can tell and am told, nothing has changed much in this industry for decades. Making matters worse today, the Financial Planning Association found that 88 percent of consumers indicated that they would not seek services from a broker if they knew the broker was not required to act in their best interests. Sad but true, industry research supports my contention that the primary challenge for this industry is that 84 *91* percent of women feel misunderstood by advisors. It's only up from here, but nobody's paying attention. To my amazement, Metropolitan Life dismantled and closed the doors of its treasured MetLife Mature Market Institute, which had been under the respected leadership of Sandra Timmermann. The institute was revered by anyone seeking up-to-date, relevant research. Has AARP's rebranding pushed such a high-quality research resource out of business? Or perhaps the Mature Market Institute just didn't fit with MetLife's mission any longer in these and future times? Why else would MetLife have closed its doors? Once again I ask, "Where are your dancing shoes?"

(If you would like more information on how you can be a rock solid advisor, and how best to serve the over-40 women's market, let me know by email, Karen@KarenSands.com, with "Rock Solid Advisors" in the subject line.) There's hope on the horizon.

Old School Male-Dominated Industries Taking a Peek

Even the auto industry is catching on. The 50-plus demographic is again having an enormous impact on American auto sales. Over the last three years, this buying age cohort contributed a startling 84 percent of the $1.5 million increase in sales.

Believe it or not, Walmart is launching a new circular designation label announcing when the company behind a product (any items from lingerie to hummus) is women-owned. Watch out, gluten-free, fair-trade, or made in America. Walmart is putting its money where its mouth is by pledging to source $20 billion of goods from "Women Owned Businesses" (WOB) in the United States by 2016. For other reasons, Walmart is not a favorite employer or retailer for me, yet they are super-savvy market strategists.

Swiffer, another cutting-edge advertiser, is so savvy it is appealing across generations. Every time I see the Swiffer ads, they make me laugh and feel warm inside. The most popular Swiffer spot is when we are invited into the Valley Stream home of a couple in their nineties, Lee and Morty Kaufman, who, with the magic of their first Swiffer, discover how much dirt and dust has been left behind from using traditional dusting and cleaning tools like brooms, mops, and even vacuums. (I'm always amazed. I still show my husband when I get a big Swiffer load!) I read the other day that Elizabeth Ming, the spokeswoman for Swiffer, confirmed my take that this spot resonates with Americans of all ages—because many consumers aspire to have a similar loving, enduring relationship. What a plug for Ageless Marketing!

You'd think other retailers would be following suit in droves, right? Yet, this trend of investing in post-50s is not only lower in the United States, but also in many other countries. So what gives?

The truth is, we are back to the conundrum of sometimes opposing pulls between profit and mission again. If you want to pay your bills and have a life, then profits win every time. Just keep an eye on the marketplace and you'll observe product designers, marketers, and service providers waking up and moving into this new story of *The Ageless Way*, albeit ever so slowly.

Higher Education Steps Up to the Plate

It's crucial for all industries and fields to reach out to the 50-plus demographic; some of the most savvy are doing so. Higher education is no exception. Both Professor Rosabeth Moss Kanter at Harvard and a spanking-new initiative at Stanford University are trawling for a new kind of student seeking to reinvent the next stage after midlife. Stanford openly espouses that it wants to attract proven leaders with twenty to thirty years of work experience on the hunt to reinvent their futures.

University and advanced adult education and professional development programs are the future. No doubt a proliferation of new higher education programs modeled off of the Harvard and Stanford programs will emerge over the next decades.

Twenty-First Century Boomtime Careers

I've been known to get rather passionate when I speak about the paucity of career changers and younger generations enrolled or even interested in the field of aging. Both are leaving money on the table and growing opportunities in the dust.

I want to rant and rave that the aging field is not all about changing bedpans. Don't get me wrong; personal care for the frail elderly and disabled is a critical task for one of the fastest growing careers today as a health care worker.

Rather, what I'm so excited about are the enormous possibilities for meaningful work in serving the maturing 40-plus market, and those succeeding generations who will soon be 40-plussers themselves. That's why in this chapter I'm compelled to include the trend information relating to new careers in aging.

Yet we continue to read and hear from the media that Millennials have no opportunities before them, or that Boomers and Millennials will continue to fight for job positions. Give me a break! There are so many untapped career opportunities in the aging field (and it's tangential fields) that no one needs to be out of work! That is, not if they are trained and skilled, especially those with a long career history.

Just take a look at the numbers: The United States Census Bureau and Civic Ventures project reports that by 2030, Americans age 55 and older will number 107.6 million, 31 percent of the population. Those over 65 will account for 20 percent of the total population. The Nielsen study reports that by 2017 Baby Boomers will control 70 percent of America's disposable income. This is a market to be reckoned with, so it's best to get on the new millennium job growth curve in the field of aging sooner rather than later. Otherwise, you may miss an incredible opportunity of these times for your career, your business, or your organization.

Please be advised that everything in the field of aging is morphing rapidly, creating an exciting plethora of emerging opportunities in a variety of specialty roles and services. Not only because of the swelling ranks of the over-50s, but because the field of aging is evolving at warp speed. It's not just bedpans anymore.

My goal here is to make sure you stay with me and not get turned off to this meaningful, high-impact field as your possible "what's next" or as your new marketplace to increase your market share. So I'm going to ask you to stay with me while I share an overview of the aging field's history right up to today…and tomorrow.

As I write, there is a great deal of healthy Creative Destruction going on in the aging field. The new "older adult" demographic of Leading-Edge Boomers is wreaking havoc on the longtime preferred and universally accepted disease model of aging that has long been the underpinning of the field.

I'm a rabid fan of transforming the language, symbolism, and narrative around aging. Our languaging, especially around hot-button topics, reveals what's not being said out loud or what is still unconscious and informs how we perceive or imagine things to be. So let's start off with the languaging, including commonly accepted definitions and how they are integrally entwined with the history of the aging field.

The Basics:
A Language and History Overview

My previous pejorative references to bedpans equating to the essence of the aging services field is a perfect example of how negative symbolism in the current narrative around careers in aging has a significantly pessimistic impact on the future of the aging field. We need a more enticing symbolism and depiction of the field of possibilities now emerging for younger generations, as well as for Baby Boomers seeking Third and Fourth Age recareering or new start-up ventures.

The more common notions people have about the field of aging are rooted in geriatrics, which is built on the disease model. Geriatrics is solely about comprehensive health care of older adults, with a focus on the study of illness and diseases of later life. For as long as I can remember, working with older adults fell into the realm of health care only.

Gerontology is the antithesis of the disease model, as it is the study of the process of aging and adult development, (emotional, psychological, spiritual and physical) across the life course and the societal implications of the impact of an aging population. Since the field of gerontology is multidisciplinary, it is a catch-all for many professionals like myself who are known as professional gerontologists. Many of us have other fields of expertise that enhance what we bring to the field and the 40-plus market. There are no limits to the creative integration of a variety of disciplines that are possible now in serving the enormous and fast-moving older adult market.

Only recently, the field of possibilities began expanding as never before. The "change-everything-in-our path" Boomer demographic is creating an insatiable market need for innovation in the development and delivery of new services and products as it heads into older and Elder adulthood. Leading-Edge Boomers are paving the way for all who follow by demanding to remain productive, independent, and active wherever they live and work. This is heaven-sent to social entrepreneurs seeking new avenues to make a difference and add to the Triple Bottom Line of People, Planet, and Profit.

Historically, academic programs in gerontology modeled the narrow worldview of geriatrics with the disease and illness model deeply embedded in the curriculum.

In 1994, when I received my post-graduate certification in Adult Development and Aging at Hunter College's Brookdale Center of Aging under the auspices of Rose Dobrof and my mentor Professor Harry R. Moody (aka Rick), our curriculum and course resources were almost all based on the geriatric disease model of aging. I almost quit the program several times because I was so done with the old paradigm. At that time, there were neither master's degrees nor Ph.D.s in gerontology being offered in the tri-state metro area, so this was my only choice. Clearly the cosmos was watching out for me once again. Dr. Moody offered me the opportunity to teach the first *Conscious Aging 101* course at a university level—a precursor of the new Positive Aging genre now growing by leaps and bounds here in the United States and around the world.

Back then, author-consultants with expertise in the 40-plus market were hard to find, many relatively unknown working on the edge of the mainstream. Emerging as new thought leaders but still in the shadows of mainstream were my mentors, teachers, and colleagues. Among them were breakthrough marketer, author, and creator of *Ageless Marketing*, David Wolfe (who turned how we market to older adults inside-out) and Ken Dychtwald, author of *Age Wave* and founder of his corporate consultancy of the same name who was, to my knowledge, the first to get Fortune 500 companies to consider the elderly as a market for consumer products and services.

I know about what was happening back then because I was one of the few visionaries sounding the clarion call to serve the emerging and burgeoning 40-plus market. Unlike the others, I also had bottom-line responsibility for producing breakthrough results and increased market share in a variety of ventures serving the emerging 40-plus market in financial services. My leadership role in securing my company's market position as the one-stop provider for retirement products and planning services propelled me into an unexpected role as the resident futurist studying the Graying of America and the world. I am forever grateful for this fortuitous opportunity to hone my skills and knowledge base as a futurist and gerontologist. Any extra time I had, I spent studying the future of women and aging, along with entrepreneurship in America for the twenty-first century.

Conscious Aging Bursts onto the Scene

Paralleling the new breed of Ageless marketing geniuses and joining these new thought leaders in the aging field were the groundbreakers in the human potential and consciousness movement. In the early 1990s, these visionaries and groundbreakers started a new movement with a vision they eloquently and improvisationally enunciated as Conscious Aging.

In 1992, the Omega Institute in Rhinebeck hosted a two-day conference in Manhattan entitled "Conscious Aging." I was one of the 1,500 attendees who found ourselves in seventh heaven finding new community while rubbing shoulders with idols like Maggie Kuhn (who in 1970 founded the Gray Panthers), Robert Atchley (a pioneer in the Conscious Aging field and author of *Social Forces and Aging,* now in its 10th edition), sharing the birthing of a new paradigm with Jungian author, teacher, and my beloved mentor, Marion Woodman, joined by spiritual leaders and authors, Ram Dass and Rabbi Zalman Schachter-Shalomi…and, of course, my deeply valued Harry (Rick) Moody still sounding the call and supporting others to keep the Positive Aging flame lit. There are other trailblazers I've met along the way, like pioneering radio show host and author of many books on caregiving, Connie Goldman, and professor-author Wendy Lustbader. I'm sure I've forgotten a few, but check these folks out so you can get a handle on what's really going on in the field of aging.

We all left the Omega conference on a high. We were carrying the message Atchley, chair of the Department of Gerontology at Naropa University in Boulder, Colorado, captured so well when he described the essence of Conscious Aging as "our intention to be awake (conscious) as we age." As a whole, those of us in attendance committed ourselves to the view that later life (I see midlife as the portal) is, at core, about our inner spiritual growth and hopefully our enlightened contribution to humanity no matter our age, cycle, or stage.

In 1994, there were a couple more of these inspiring events, but as outspoken Atchley decries, convening conferences is a bottom-line business, so profits won out over mission, leaving the Conscious Aging community to be nomadic, splintered for a long time.

Positive Aging Eclipses Conscious Aging

Approximately a decade ago, a new conference convened, reconfiguring our community around the concept of Positive Aging. The first of its kind, the Positive Aging Conference was hosted at Eckerd College, St. Petersburg, Florida, in 2007. The second conference migrated to the University of Minnesota's Center for Spirituality and Healing, then back to Eckerd for the third conference. In 2010, the conference moved west to Los Angeles, California, under the esteemed hosting of the Fielding Graduate University's Institute for Social Innovation, where the next three sterling conferences were held. Upcoming hosts are the Society of Certified Senior Advisors and Fielding University. Fortunately this conference will continue to reach more of us as it moves to different hosts, bringing us together to sound the clarion call for Positive Aging.

What's Next for Positive Aging?

Perhaps Atchley is spot-on when he concludes that "if we seek a wider audience, we experience commercial pressures from promoters and publishers to make our efforts fit within their models." I'm all for monetizing our visions, but as of yet we have not found a successful formula for convening this cutting-edge community of professionals together. I'm holding on to the vision that our niche professional community will rally and come together again. The Positive Aging story is incomplete as we again splinter into myriad smaller gatherings, some online and some off.

No matter what happens around how or when we convene again, I'm thrilled to be part of a growing generation of new thought leaders in the field of aging who are ushering in a new Positive Aging paradigm. This new paradigm is breaking up what was, while in its place it is birthing an organic, unlimited holistic view of the life course and of our unlimited, as yet untapped, human potential available to us as we age.

New scenarios are developing around the concept of Positive Aging. This meme is disrupting our old story of aging in every aspect of our lives. Savvy marketers and social entrepreneurs are getting hip to what's trending now…and into the future. This space is ripe for innovation. The top tier of corporate America (unlike the UK and Asia) has not yet taken serious notice. This is the time to jump in—feet first, for the nimble visionary few, before the many soon-to-catch on will stampede this space. There is growing interest in measuring, tracking and evaluating the behavior and needs (real and perceived) of the the forty-plus demographic. Perfect opportunity for newbie and encore startups. At the same time, 40-plussers are also directly impacting innovation for all ages by demanding products that are age-friendly on a variety of fronts, e.g., from products and services needed, to new delivery solutions, an workforce development and encore careers and new start-ups.

Why You Need to Know about Educational Gerontology

A longtime respected name in the field attended my "Visionaries Have Wrinkles" talk at the 2014 Positive Aging Conference. Afterward, she came up to introduce herself. While chatting and exchanging tales about the field and how we arrived on this career path, she described herself as an "educational gerontologist." I had not heard that term before in my advanced training programs, so I asked her what the term means as a career. I got a hearty laugh as she told me, "Karen, you too are an educational gerontologist." I just didn't know there's a name for what I have been doing my entire adult career!

When I got back to my hotel room, I Googled "educational gerontology." What I found is that David A. Peterson in 1976 introduced the definition of educational gerontology, which I'll paraphrase as the study and practice of instructional activities for and about the aged and aging. For me, it was enlightening to find an umbrella for what I do within the aging field, which as Ronald H. Sherron and D. Barry Lumsden (in their 1990 third edition textbook, *Introduction to Educational Gerontology*), state "to prevent premature decline, to facilitate meaningful roles, and to encourage psychological growth." In translation, they describe what I do, and what educational gerontology is about, "designed as a positive approach to helping people better understand and assist themselves." I was thrilled to read that Howard McClusky, 1971, shaped the definition that resonates with me as a "positive domain" in which the potential of the individual is accepted and developed in order to ensure continuing growth throughout the life span. For years I've struggled with how to define what my work in the field of aging is. I need look no longer!

Age Rush: Crisis and Opportunity

Now for the challenges facing the aging field.

Educational Gerontology

Much like the underfunded Positive Aging and Conscious Aging conferences of the past, my research has uncovered that many of the academic gerontology programs at universities and colleges around the United States are also experiencing dwindling enrollment and difficulties in contributing to their institutions' balance sheets. The downswing in registration and enrollment are putting these programs on notice, and some may end up on the chopping block as no longer viable.

How the Great Recession Affected Higher Education

Let's start with a look at how the Great Recession impacted higher education in general. Harvard's Jeffrey Brown and Caroline Hoxby, eds., in their 2013 revised paper, "How the Great Recession Affected Higher Education," conclude that the Great Recession had far-reaching effects on both the supply and demand sides of higher education. Based on the analysis of the Integrated Postsecondary Education Data System

(IPEDS), an annual survey of colleges (2014), it appears that college enrollment and attendance levels increased during the Great Recession, "especially in the states most affected by the recession. Part-time enrollment increased while full-time enrollment declined, and the gains in attendance were concentrated among students of color. In addition, the authors share that "The tuition revenue collected per student also grew, while grants did not offset the increase in cost and student loans increased." The authors referenced the study by Dellas and Sakellaris (2003) in which they concluded, "college enrollment decisions are countercyclical with the business cycle."

Conundrum: Something Is Not Quite Right

So if enrollment tends to rise in poor economic times, why is it that enrollment and attendance in gerontology programs is on the decline…or, as has been suggested to me, why is it that some programs have prospered while others are declining?

According to a review article on the survival of small college gerontology programs, Drs. Ronald Lucchino and K. Della Ferguson, the director and assistant director, respectively, for what was then the Institute of Gerontology of Syracuse University, conclude that small colleges are "currently undergoing a squeeze between a decline in students and a reduction in federal support." The authors claim these downward changes translate directly into "reduced resources to support academic programs and community initiatives."

Could it be my bedpan analogy again? Methinks gerontology careers and, by default, educational gerontology, have a branding image problem. Clearly there's a language barrier.

Even the name of the field causes folks' eyes to glaze over, to defer to the youth market. More difficult to dismantle is our shared deeply ingrained image of what aging is and how we envision it. For most, it's of no interest, or just not relevant.

There's more. It comes back to profit over mission. Are we as a nation and global economies willing to risk the elimination or curtailment of gerontology programs at all levels, from certifications to doctorates? Doing so would mean that serving the growing population of people over 40 would no longer be a vital part of our higher education programming.

That's nuts in my book! The current and continuing record growth of employment opportunities for graduates with gerontological training brought on by the "graying of America," and the "graying of the globe" is where it's at for employment growth. The increasing demand for new and upgraded services, as well as product and delivery systems built around a techno-savvy older consumer, is growing rapidly, benefitting all of us now and when we are 40-plus.

Labor force projections indicate that large numbers of additional professional personnel will be needed to serve this tidal wave of older people, especially women service providers and entrepreneurs. I'm not referring to only health care or bedpan changing, but myriad career and entrepreneurial opportunities in related fields and industries where gerontological knowledge is greatly valued and sought after. Examples of opportunities include cutting-edge age-friendly technology and devices, home design and architecture, smart electronics, adult education, and many emerging services catering to the unique needs of 40-plussers as well as addressing the universal needs of all consumers.

Here are some things you may not yet know about. The current number of health care providers and social workers trained in gerontology is totally inadequate, and there's not a doubt in my mind that the demand is going to increase more quickly than we can train and hire new professionals. From my survey of curricula, faculty expertise, and program and university resources available across the United States, it's clear to me that most programs do not have sufficient up-to-date content nor educational resources required to keep demanding Boomers and fast-learning Millennials matriculating, much less entering the aging field. What a missed opportunity all around!

By no means is the Boomer bubble going to become a blip in time. Fifty-plusser Boomtime is here to stay—with the forty-plusser boontime right along side. Wake-up call: The first Gen Xers turned 50 in 2015.

Please don't be myopic or hesitate because you don't want to make waves. There's a humongous "happening" now that will continue to expand opportunities for older and younger students to acquire or upgrade their gerontological knowledge and skills so they, and we, have an enviable advantage as a wage earner, top honcho at the helm, savvy investor, innovative business owner and/or consumer. This is a long-lasting next Gold Rush. Now is the time to educate and up-skill, so you are in demand. No matter what your ideal work or give back role is, this "gray is the new green" field of possibilities will impact you both directly and indirectly. Why not make it yours? (You can read more about this in chapter two, "The Longevity Economy.")

Our higher educational institutions must cater to careers in aging, as well as offer adult learning and continuing lifelong education. Demand is so high that more and more gerontology certificate programs are showing up at the undergraduate level. Then there is the range of gerontology degrees available at various colleges and universities (e.g., associate, bachelor's, master's, and more recently Ph.D. degrees). Add to this list an assortment of professional certifications like Certified Senior Advisor, Certified Age-Friendly or Aging-in-Place Specialist, Business and Aging Specialist, Certified Financial Planner, and on and on. These certifications are becoming standard fare faster and faster to fill the exploding need. At the same time, professional certifications and credentialing are becoming more mainstream, gaining in popularity with students of all ages and acceptance by industry and consumers. These new professional certifications are popping up all over, giving educational institutions new competition.

Bottom Line

There is an unprecedented opportunity rising to the top of every industry's consumer landscape. To be successful in the anti-aging, luxury-brand women's market today, a company must address the specific needs, buying patterns, and attitudes of Boomer women who account for 95 percent of the purchase decisions for their households.

Modern-Day Story Conflicts and You

For those going through life stage shifts, particularly at midlife and beyond, these greater societal shifts and story conflicts run parallel to the transitions and upheaval in our personal and professional lives. The chaos and uncertainty is coming from all sides, and it's tempting to hang on for dear life to anything stable and certain we can find, even if doing so means remaining in an unfulfilling career or toxic work environment, such as what former BBC presenter, Miriam O'Reilly (53) experienced. O'Reilly was one of four female presenters, all in their forties or fifties, who were dropped from the 23-year-old show. Not only did she leave…she filed an age-discrimination and victimization suit and won.

These are the times when we have more opportunities, not fewer, to transform our work, our world, and ourselves.

A fast-moving wave of a diverse cross-section of us is leaving behind the hallowed halls of large corporations, institutions, and organizations. No matter how you leave one chapter to the next, the *no-exit* terror of those *no-return* revolving doors as you make your way out are anxiety-producing, even frightening, especially in chaotic times. We are in the midst of a page-turner. We are witnessing, and are morphing into, lean and mean new start-ups. Clearly our feminine entrepreneurial spirit is rising.

The new breed of entrepreneurs is primarily women, remarkably powerful, savvy, experienced Boomer women—most of us social entrepreneurs going for the Triple Bottom Line: People, Planet, and Profit. We are well connected and ready to rock. We can maximize our capabilities, get greater reach and scope, to serve exiting and emerging markets. To me, the most exciting of these are women-to-women networks of women serving one another. Perfect for Baby Boomers and the younger generations moving forward.

BBC News reports that among United States encore entrepreneurs, women are actually more prevalent than men. Babson College, a Boston-area business school with a highly regarded entrepreneurial program, reported in 2010 that 10 percent of U.S. women aged between 55 and 64 had taken steps to start their own businesses, compared with 7.5 percent of men. By 2030, it is expected that at least 18 percent of the U.S. population will be 65 or older. That's at a rate of ten thousand people turning 65 every day in the United States alone.

Now is the time of small business and solopreneurship. For others, it's perhaps time for reinvigorating and evolving existing businesses or taking careers full steam ahead. The old story is being rewritten by significant advancements and shifts in technology, financing, and corporate culture, which are rippling out to make more and more of us reinvent our businesses and ourselves.

The human brain naturally seeks patterns and order, especially in chaos. The bigger the problems we need to solve, the bigger the innovations we create. When the world around us is orderly and certain, we tend to think inside that same box that is serving us so well. But when the world around us is falling apart and that box has been torn to shreds, we have no choice but to think outside it, creating new connections by drawing together seemingly disparate ideas from the chaotic whirlwind that surrounds us. This is the idea behind Bucky Fuller's concept of "emergence through emergency," that most times it takes an emergency, such as on the scale of climate change, for our best selves to emerge collectively and act in innovative ways. In the 1960s the emergencies included the assassinations of JFK and MLK, the Vietnam War protests, civil rights marches, and the Second Wave Feminist movement. Now the emergencies are squeezing out the middle class, causing potential planetary demise, allowing big business to gain a stranglehold on politics, triggering barbaric international terrorism, exposing stateside police brutality, and more.

There is a reason mythology tends to personify destruction and creation in one being, such as in the Hindu goddess Kali and the Buddhist goddess Kuan Yin, and the Egyptian goddess Isis. The two ideas go hand in hand. Where there is destruction, there is a powerful drive to create something new. Sometimes, creation requires destruction—destroying the habits and limited ways of thinking that stand in the way of forging new paths, for example. Now, we refer to this phenomenon as "Creative Destruction." More often, innovation relies on selective destruction, getting rid of what no longer serves us without losing what does. Just as our Mother Earth depends more and more on recycling and creating something new by reworking the old, transformation that leads to sustainable success and innovation often depends on new combinations.

Now, more than ever, you have the opportunity to go beyond temporary solutions and quick fixes toward sustainable game-changing ideas that could alter your life, your work, and the world in ways only you can imagine. The future belongs to those who are starting those transformations now, who are reshaping or shaping the world and creating their own place in it. For example, take the new smartphones with bigger screens and adjustable fonts. They are perfect for enabling the enormous audience of over-40s who are beginning to feel the vision pinch to stay connected. Or consider Eyebobs, the high-fashion mid-priced reading magnifiers that are pretty and utilitarian. Just perfect for the 40-plus women's market. I recently came across another example when I met with a Millennial female founder of an online start-up built on an amalgamation of several business models and platforms. For her, it all started as she headed for an important high-fashion business event overseas. The suddenly cold and wet weather of her destination country put her in a quandary as her travel wardrobe was unsuitable for the inclement weather. She was forced to buy an expensive high-fashion coat, which she'd rarely use again. Frustrated, she was determined to come up with a solution for women on the go to avoid having to spend a fortune on such emergency, infrequently worn, or one-time outfits. Now, this fashion diva is growing her win-win exchange platform whereby a combination of high fashion, recycling, and consignment short-term rentals is available online. The takeaway from this story is that opportunity is all around us, if we just look with non-judgmental beginner's eyes.

A Future That Works

If you can't afford to make a huge leap now—starting or reinvigorating your own business, changing or reinventing your career, transforming your organization—you can, and should, start doing the legwork now so that, when the opportunity presents itself, you'll be on firm footing to make that leap with confidence, without hesitation.

Staying on top of trends can help you lead change with your ideas, instead of being swept along by it uncontrollably. As I describe in chapter one, we can all step into the role of modern-day oracles, connecting the realities of the present story with probable futures. We can then see which of those preferred futures we aspire to and begin to make steps to create our own self-fulfilling prophecies.

The trends you analyze will depend somewhat on your personal and professional interests, experiences, goals, and vision. For most of us, however, having an idea of where the world of work is likely to go is crucial to creating a future that integrates what matters most to us and how we want to spend our time with what the world wants and needs. We need to know what story we are currently in and what stories are possible if we are going to create our ideal aspirational story. In other words, knowing something about the likely future of work will help us to create a future that works—for all of us.

Each and every one of us can tease out a through line within our stories that intersects with an emerging trend or trends, as I have over and over again as a serial entrepreneur. The same is true to the max with Katy Fike. In her own words, Fike, formerly an investment banker with Lehman Brothers, shares what propelled her into the field of aging, caring, and technology as a youngster: "I was just seven years old when my ninety-year-old grandmother moved in with my family after breaking her hip. I witnessed firsthand many of the issues still faced by caregivers and elderly individuals across the country." As a result, Fike is now the founder and CEO of INNOVATE50 Consulting LLC and co-founder of Aging2.0, a global innovation network.

Consider these trends:

- The United States Department of Labor estimates that the number of information-technology jobs is expected to grow at more than twice the overall job-growth rate. These jobs include knowledge work, an area that has been growing explosively for years now, such as jobs related to software, problem solving and strategy, communications and networks, and various careers in math and science.

- Health care, education—anything related to the enormous gray market—are expected to continue being reliable areas of job growth, especially as the large generation of Baby Boomers continues to age. By 2022, the estimated job growth in personal care and home health workers is expected to be up to 50 percent of the current market. Health care and age-friendly home modification will grow exponentially.

- The business world is finally realizing that it can save money by offering leadership, team, and individual executive coaching, and by promoting work-life balance, flexible work arrangements, and collaborative business models. For example, telecommuting can save businesses real estate and payroll costs. Reduced hours, unpaid sabbaticals, lateral employee movements (such as from one department to another) without any of this sidelining employee career growth are more cost-effective than laying off employees and having to start from scratch as the economy improves.

- Baby Boomers and succeeding generations will be working past traditional retirement age (at least nine years, according to T. Rowe Price), some for financial reasons and others because they simply have no desire to retire. The flexible arrangements mentioned above will come into play, such as more job sharing, even at senior levels, as well as more Boomers filling the need for knowledge workers as strategists, consultants, and coaches—not to mention as entrepreneurs.

- Companies will be hiring more and more women in all positions, including senior management. Women executives and board members tend to lead to higher returns, and the cost-saving measures described above have their roots in the collaborative management style and emphasis on work-life balance introduced in many businesses by female leadership. The coming gap between college graduates and the need for college-educated workers will be filled primarily by women, who earn more college and advanced degrees than men do.

- Women already control 85 percent of consumer spending in the United States. They are the present and future market for businesses worldwide. Boomer women in particular have spending clout. Businesses who ignore this market of Ageless Women and continue to portray us in ways that are not relevant to our preferred futures do so at significant risk of losing a huge market share.

- Boomers and Millennials in general are choosing to spend their money based on their values, such as purchasing from green companies.

- The aging field is growing at a rapid pace as more and more people require aging-related services, mainly women, simply because they tend to outlive men. Now more than ever, women can make a dent in this growing market, no matter which field or career path leads them to serving one another and themselves. I foresee and relish a model of "women-to-women" businesses emerging to serve the needs and desires of the enormous 40-plus market, especially women serving other women and being paid well to do so.

Whatever your vision for the future, these trends can help you determine the shape of it. First, consider the story you are currently telling yourself about your work, your ideal customers or clients, your future. How do these trends change that story?

As an entrepreneur, consider what these facts and probable events tell you about what you have to offer, what your audience needs and wants, your options for hiring and outsourcing, and how you can create a business model that combines purpose and profit for sustainable success that also makes a difference in the world.

As a leader in your organization, you have the opportunity to create win-win situations for the company and the people you lead by being among the first to make changes that lead to more profit, happier and more productive employees, greater loyalty among your customers, and improved products and services for the market of today and of the future, all while increasing your bottom line.

As a professional looking to change careers or to transform how you work—because you are approaching retirement age or wanting to devote more time and energy to what really matters—these trends can show you many scenarios and their relative risks and benefits, as well as spark your own reimagining of your personal and professional life. When you have the alternative stories laid out and grounded in reality, you can better see which narrative you wish to create with your tomorrows. In other words, you can change your story when you are happy with the probable ending.

Don't be afraid to think outside the statistical box, either. Sure, you could look at the aging Boomer population and think about the need for more senior living communities and nursing homes, or you could look at what this community needs and wants and strike out in a novel direction that offers an alternative to these kinds of places or that recognizes how this generation is likely to turn stereotypes about aging on their head. For example, there is an emerging interest in creating communal intergenerational living situations based on shared values rather than grouping Elders together regardless of whether they have anything in common besides their age.

Of course, looking at trends is only one small part of an overall strategy for reinventing your future. But this is an action you can start taking today, even if you feel trapped in your current situation. You may not feel in control of your present, yet your future is entirely in your hands. The new green is your opportunity to monetize the future by applying an Aspirational Ageless Approach to "PrimeTime Women." ❯

CHAPTER 1 ~ *Reflections*

The questions and exercises below are to help you find your distinct path to rocking your revenues in the Longevity Economy. Turn to page vii for more about the Gray is the New Green Reflections.

1. Take each of the trends mentioned in this chapter (also read more in chapter two, "The Longevity Economy") and write down how each affects you now. How might each trend affect you in the future? What can you do to leverage the trends in your professional life, existing business, by volunteering, or in a new start-up?

2. Here are a few trigger questions to apply to each trend to get you started thinking way outside the box:

3. How might this trend influence your current customers?

4. How might this trend influence your core business?

5. How does this trend impact your current and future workforce and workplace?

6. How might this trend attract new customers?

7. What are your two closest competitors doing about this trend?

8. Are there other trends co-evolving with this one?

9. How fast is this trend developing and what might accelerate it or slow it down?

10. How is your business reaching and serving the 40-plus market?

11. If you are planning to leave your job or sell your business, have you formulated an exit strategy?

12. What is your business doing to change with the needs of 40-plus existing and potential customers? What about your current colleagues and employees?

13. How are you getting your organization or your one-woman show ready for the prime-time Boomer women challenge and turning it into a humongous opportunity? What can you start now to leverage the 40-plus trend?

14. What and who needs to change so you and your business or organization can leverage this prime-time Boomer women trend?

15. What is your vision and intended outcome relative to each trend?

16. What are the three top challenges you face or your most pressing questions you have about serving the 40-plus market and, more specifically, in serving "PrimeTime Women?" Please contact me if you would like to discuss this further. Send your email to Karen@KarenSands.com, with "GNG Challenges" in the subject line.

Chapter 2

THE LONGEVITY ECONOMY

I won't step aside.
We are not going to play dead
'cause we are a "certain age."

~ Cher, 2014

What Is The Longevity Economy?

Before we move on, I want to respond to a query I'm often asked: "Why do you prefer to focus on the forty-plus segment versus solely focusing on fifty-plus, especially Baby Boomers?" My response is much the same as David Wolfe's on this topic, as he describes the future of the Ageless Market: "Markets over forty will grow at a far faster clip than markets under forty."

This changes everything. Marketing and sales become all about serving the Ageless Market, principally Ageless Women.

As you are well aware now, the 50-plus demographic is an unstoppable powerful force for change, which is impacting the United States economy, as well as most other economies, and will for generations to come.

The group of "oldies but goodies" now 50-plus are expected to represent 54 percent of the over-25 population by 2032. With thirty more years now added to expected lifespans, this group is morphing everything in its path as it moves from an elongated productive midlife into a later and later onset of old old age. A briefing paper prepared for AARP by Oxford Economics states that this force of older people in the United States alone is composed of 106 million people responsible for at least $7.1 trillion in annual economic activity—a figure that is expected to reach well over $13.5 trillion in real terms by 2032.

It is important to note that the Longevity Economy isn't just defined by demographics. This term also applies to the total of all economic activity related to serving the needs of the post-40s in the United States, as well as the products and services this same demographic purchases directly and the continued economics their spending engenders.

Echoing my own take on the Longevity Economy, the briefing report concludes that this is not a passing phenomenon. Long after we 40-plussers are past tense, longer and longer life spans will result in continuously occurring large post-40 populations.

I want to share another striking and telling statistic from the briefing paper that nails the import and impact of this new economic trend "The over-50 population controls almost 80% of U.S. aggregate net worth; the average wealth of households headed by people over 50 is almost three times the size of those headed by people aged 25 to 50."

The Effect of Longevity on Our Future Economy

We know that living longer, healthier lives, coupled with the sheer numbers of the aging Boomer population, presents us all with a financial challenge. How do we make our money last as long as we do?

Sound financial planning is an obvious answer. It's also an ideal-world answer. In the real world, the aftereffects of the Great Recession, the costs of caring for parents and children, and the denial of the eventual effects of aging on our health are just a few factors that can make financial planning insufficient to secure the future.

For many, the solution is to work past traditional retirement age, some by necessity but many others out of a desire to keep working. Individuals and companies are catching on to the idea of flexible working options, particularly those that allow telecommuting, job sharing, and shorter workweeks. These are benefits not just for Boomers but for the younger working generations as well.

Most age-friendly ideas for the workplace (and indeed for our homes and communities) are beneficial to all ages and stages. The sooner organizations and governments recognize this growing customer demand (and the more we emphasize it), the more prosperous and secure we will all be, in the workplace and as a nation.

In fact, longevity has been shown to have a positive effect on the economy. This is indeed the new story of our times. A 2005 study, "The Value of Health and Longevity," by Robert

Topel and Kevin Murphy, of the University of Chicago Booth School of Business, demonstrates massive economic benefit to living longer and healthier than in the past:

> *Over the 20th century, cumulative gains in life expectancy were worth over $1.2 million per person for both men and women. Between 1970 and 2000 increased longevity added about $3.2 trillion per year to national wealth, an uncounted value equal to about half of average annual GDP over the period. Reduced mortality from heart disease alone has increased the value of life by about $1.5 trillion per year since 1970. The potential gains from future innovations in health care are also extremely large. Even a modest 1 percent reduction in cancer mortality would be worth nearly $500 billion.*

Therein lies the paradox: Longevity is undeniably good for the economy as a whole, while presenting economic challenges for the individual. How do we bring the economic benefits to the individual?

This question is crucial not only for Baby Boomers but also for future generations, especially the massive (80 million-plus) Millennial generation. We need more than short-term fixes. We need lasting changes in the workplace as well as changes in how we—at the individual, organizational, and governmental level—ensure a financial safety net that is adequate for the longer lives many of us will have. The Longevity Economy is the new story for our future, but it's up to us to shape that story for our families, the world, and ourselves.

Retiring Retirement

One of the first steps we need to take is to re-evaluate retirement, especially as a default assumption at an arbitrary age. This seemingly picked-out-of-a-hat age demarcation hit home for me particularly when I was reading an article about retirement age, and how it has changed and is changing. All I could think was, "What difference does it make?"

Why do we even have a "retirement age"? Maybe in the past, a particular age could be associated with a time when people were physically and mentally ill-equipped to continue working, so this age provided them with some guarantee of health care and continued income (although I would argue that this arbitrary age was never accurate and perhaps contributed to a dangerous myth that kept people from fulfilling their true potential beyond midlife).

Do you wonder why we have a mandatory retirement age? Right out of the United States rule book of federal legislation, "mandatory retirement," also known as "enforced retirement," is the set age at which people who hold certain jobs or offices are required by industry custom or by law to leave their employment, or retire. Typically, mandatory retirement is justified by the argument that certain occupations are either too dangerous (military personnel) or require high levels of physical and mental skill (air-traffic controllers, airline pilots). Most mandatory retirement decisions rely on the notion that a worker's productivity declines significantly after age 65, or now age 70, and the mandatory retirement is the employer's way to avoid reduced productivity. Of course nowadays, an employer can no longer force retirement or otherwise discriminate on the basis of age against an individual because he or she is 70 or older.

But today, we know that people are living longer, healthier, more active lives across the board. You've heard that 60 is the new 40 (and 70 the new 50, 80 the new 60, etc.). This isn't just a marketing slogan. We all look around at our friends, our families, ourselves, and we know this is superficially true. Yet I would argue that the deeper truth is that 60 is the new 60. Who we are inside has earned every year of our existence. Why downplay even a single year that has shaped who we are?

No matter which way you look at it, it doesn't make any sense to be quibbling about a few years here and there in a person's sixties. What kind of sense does it make to be thinking about a retirement age for someone who is functionally in her forties yet with the experience and wisdom of her full sixty years? Or conversely?

And when you really start thinking about what "retirement age" means, what kind of sense does it make, period?

The only valuable purpose I can see for having this demarcation at all is to be sure everyone in our society is taken care of when they are not as equipped to care for themselves. Isn't this an ideal for people of any age? If health or disability interferes with a person's ability to provide for him or herself, does it really matter whether the person is 65 or 25?

So that leaves Social Security, which we've all been paying into. Yes, it does make sense for this fund to be available as we age because it is true that at some point we will be less able to work as much as before (even if we keep working). It is true that the longer we live, the more likely part of our income will go increasingly toward health-related expenses. But what on earth does this reality have to do with retirement?

I'm not talking about denying age. Just the opposite. I'm talking about looking at the realities of aging for what they really are, and this includes what they are not. The old stories about aging are simply not true for us. Aging does not equal retiring. It does not mean we step back and sit on our rocking chairs while the younger folks take over. We may want or need to work less, or to have more flexible working arrangements, but think about that: Don't we all need that at every age?

A young parent who needs to be able to work from home or work more flexible hours and a 70-year-old who needs the same arrangement are functionally equivalent. A 40-year-old who wants to "retire early," meaning she wants to stop working for someone else and pursue her own interests, be they travel or entrepreneurship or both, is no different from an 80-year-old who wants the same thing.

"Retirement age" and similar phrases, in other words, lump together a bunch of characteristics and needs and wants that really don't have much to do with age at all. People of any age may wish to "retire"—even for just a phase of life, before returning or starting a new career. People of any age may need flexibility and help because of a health- or disability-related crisis or ongoing situation. People of any age may wish to never retire in any sense of the word, not even at 90 or 100. They want to keep working and creating and leading. They simply need to make adaptations in these pursuits that take into account the realities of their lives—just as we all need to do, at every age.

- What if organizations, academia, families, and local and national government start looking at the needs and wants of society on an individual basis rather than lumping us by age?

- What if flexible work arrangements become the norm—for whoever wants or needs them?

- What if lifelong learning is implemented and sponsored in every nook and cranny of society—for all ages?

- What if we seek ways for those with health and disability issues (their own, their parents', their children's, their spouse's) to adapt their lives without worry, without having to give up entirely on the idea of doing what they want to do in life and giving back to society through their work, their creations, their leadership?

I believe strongly that these are all key elements to the new story of our times. This Aspirational Ageless Future may sound utopian, but it is actually a pragmatic approach to economic growth, national well-being, investment in the future, and innovation that could save us all and the planet (not to mention individual happiness). The approach is pragmatic in that it is based on doing away with stereotypes about aging, myths that keep huge numbers of people from contributing to society in unimaginable ways simply because they've hit an arbitrary number. The approach is pragmatic because it means implementing policies based on reality.

The reality is, there is no such thing as a retirement age. I doubt there ever was. We've reached the end of that old story. It's time for a new story, one created by each of us that eliminates the need for a mandatory retirement age. To do so will in turn expand a new Ageless story for all of us.

Another wrinkle for women to consider when it comes to retiring is that if you are expecting to retire to have more time to spend with your friends, think again. Today.com caught my attention with an article entitled "Women Working Longer Will Change the Face of an Aging Workforce." Apparently, if we are looking forward to retiring to have more time with friends, we are in for a shock. The article referred to a study by BLS Data, in which BLS found that the share of older women remaining in the workforce has increased sharply over the past twenty years (interestingly much more quickly than for men). BLS is projecting that women will account for 82 percent of the over-55 workforce by 2022.

The Multigenerational Workplace

All over the media we hear constant discussion about the possible growing rift between the generations as younger people are (or simply feel they are) being edged out of the workforce or promotions by the over-55 crowd. Many people in all generations take for granted as fact that every person who chooses not to retire is essentially taking a job from a younger person. Knowing it's a myth doesn't necessarily heal the anxieties overnight, especially to those who are still unemployed or underemployed. We need a new story to replace the old.

We know that, for the most part, experienced workers are filling positions that younger workers are not qualified for, simply because the younger workers haven't had the time to build the necessary skills, experience, and specialized knowledge. On the other hand, there certainly is a growing trend in hiring people over 60 for retail and similar jobs because of the perception that they will be more responsible than a younger employee. Even if they require a higher wage, the savings in training costs alone, a problem plaguing high-turnover service jobs, can be worth it. Therefore, even though the idea of older people taking jobs from younger people is as a whole not true, there are exceptions that are very real and consequential to some. We have to address the full picture if we are going to close the generational rift, however much of it is a media-manufactured story.

Focusing on ways to get more people to retire, under the belief that this will free up jobs for subsequent generations, is a mistake. Even if it were realistic, which it's not (as I note above—eschewing retirement is a trend that will only continue to grow), increasing the numbers of people receiving retirement benefits would offset the possible gains in youth employment.

Here's a show-stopper U.S. Department of Labor statistic that shocks me and might do the same for you: As recently as 2015, most members of the American workforce will be in their twenties. Sarah Sladek, CEO of XYZ University, a Minnesota-based consulting company, says it like it is: "Many companies—even industries—are in danger of 'aging out' because they haven't been able to appeal to younger generations."

So what can we do about this situation, particularly about the possibility of increasing conflict and distance among generations over perceived and real job competition? Instead of futile attempts to restore a status quo that no longer works, we can take this relatively new energy, both the negative and the positive, and re-story our present and our preferred future. Together, all generations can eliminate the generational divide, increase productivity and, thereby, we can create a new story for a future that works for all of us.

Primarily, we need to communicate with one another about it. This step seems obvious, but how often do the generations really talk about this situation? It tends to get talked about through politicians and the media rather than in collaborative, hands-on, deliberately multigenerational conversations. The World Café model (www.theworldcafe.com) is a particularly effective way of holding productive and meaningful conversations among people with seemingly disparate perspectives in any setting—businesses, homes, schools, and communities.

However we hold these conversations, they are crucial not only to get our fears and perceptions out in the open, but also to clear up the misconceptions that can lead us all to make decisions based on incorrect information or assumptions.

Second, we need to explore alternative scenarios and solutions together based on the probable and the preferred future, not the past. Now is the time to create a new story together, an aspirational future story for all of us. Yes, Social Security was an effective solution to many problems that stemmed from the Great Depression (the devastating global economic crisis that began approximately with the stock market crash in October 1929 and continued through most of the 1930s), and it continues to be a necessary element in our economy, but pursuing ways to once again push millions of post-65 people out of the workforce is not going to work. Being 65 today is not even close to what it was in that era.

Third, we should look at generational partnerships, such as job sharing/mentorship arrangements, that enable two people to be employed instead of one, enable training costs and salary to combine, stretching a company's dollar and quickening the pace at which younger employees can gain the skills, knowledge, and some of the experience they need to be more valuable to that company and the marketplace. These arrangements could work with a shifting percentage of time, starting with the mentor working three-quarters of the job, then gradually decreasing to one-half, then one-quarter, with an ultimate shift into mentoring another employee or into a consultant arrangement.

Which brings me to my fourth and final point. We need to encourage people over 60 (and in fact over 40 and 50) to remain employed by starting their own businesses. These could be less complex solopreneur home offices or larger operations that would not only remove the competition for the same job between two generations but would also generate employment.

Encore entrepreneurs, those of us over 50, are on the rise. In fact, AARP notes that folks ages 55 to 64 between 1996 through 2012 have a higher rate of new business start-ups than those ages 20 to 34.

Ken and Maddy Dychtwald of *Age Wave* fame, both authors, consultants and top-notch speakers, have long been preaching the gospel to corporate moguls and their boards about meeting the needs of our aging populace. Marc Freedman, author and founding inspiration for Encore.org, asks his audiences (as I do), "What are people in their fifties, sixties, and seventies going to do with the next thirty years of their lives?" This same question is where I started from, too, but what's at stake now is much larger…it's hard to grasp the enormity of these questions until we acknowledge that not only does this apply to almost 80 million Baby Boomers here in the United States, (the Leading Edge of which are already into their sixties and heading toward 70), but in the years to come the numbers of Millennials will overshadow those of the Boomers. It blows me away whenever I stop to ponder the enormous impact each of the generations now here on the Earth have and will have on shaping the future. For as each upcoming generation ages, these questions will be re-asked again and again…long after most of us reading this book are gone.

Ageless Workplaces

The new reality is that our employees and leaders will be working until we die. A report by the British trends consultancy The Future Laboratory, supports my view that in time more and more employees will want to age in place, but in the workplace. Let's face the facts. It's not just Baby Boomers who have another good twenty to thirty years of being productive and adding value; our current 40-somethings have the option of working at least another thirty to forty years more if they choose to do so. The Future Laboratory's findings point to a growing trend in which most of us will continue to work into old age; thus, our workplaces will morph into a new form, an Ageless Workplace! Clearly it's time to retread forced retirement into voluntary "returnment."

The future of the marketplace (and the world) lies in the rapidly growing values-based business model. People are now spending their money consciously, choosing to buy from companies that are making a difference in the world over those that aren't. More often than not, these are small, women-led businesses, the emerging new "Boomer Women Mean Business" story. Increasing numbers of these Boomer-led enterprises are supported by Ageless Women of all ages.

The Boomer Values Realignment Study adds great insight into the new Boomer generational priorities and shifting mind-set. Baby Boomers have come full circle. Well, almost. The Boomer Values Realignment Study recently showed that the Boomer reaction to the economic downturn and other national and global crises has been to focus more on relation-ships. The authors of the study refer to this as "a big shift from consumerism to relationships" as Boomers turn inward and focus more on what really matters. But this isn't an "I don't care too much for money" attitude by any means. The study also showed that Boomers care enough about money to bargain hunt and develop more thrifty spending habits. What's more, the renewed focus on meaning has affected *where* they spend their money—Baby Boomers are more likely to purchase from companies that are in line with their own values, as well as companies that will enhance their relationships with family and friends. For example, as the study shows the following:

- Ninety percent want their home to be an enticing gathering place for family and friends.

- Eighty-six percent desire a vacation connecting them with family and friends.

- Eighty-five percent are interested in a home with a smaller carbon footprint and lower operating costs.

- Eighty-three percent believe companies need to focus more on long-term growth than on short-term profits.

What do these numbers mean for businesses, especially entrepreneurs? Baby Boomers, on the whole, have $2.1 trillion in annual buying power, according to the MetLife Mature Market Institute, under the brilliant leadership of Sandra Timmerman. Many Boomers have no intention of retiring anytime soon, or they are planning retirement on their own terms with a flexible schedule and the ability to pursue what matters most to them, including building businesses based on their values (encore careers). Odds are, you are (or will be) one of them.

The shift toward a focus on relationships couldn't be more perfectly timed, as technology has changed the marketplace to be dependent on multiple networks connecting people around the world in almost infinite ways. Not only that, the market is savvy. People want more than just a connection, even with people they will never meet in person. They expect that connection to be genuine.

In the aftermath of the Great Recession, it can seem like the worst possible time to focus your business on your values, on the quality of your relationships with your clients rather than on the quantity. But the opposite is true. Baby Boomers are an indication of how your clients are changing. Living your values and focusing on what matters in your business is not only what you need, but it's what the world needs—and it's what the world is willing to pay for.

News flash: As Baby Boomers' needs change, so will the employment picture, and the very services and products available to serve the emerging needs of this generation…and all future 40-plussers.

At the same time that the Longevity Economy is demanding a new business model to serve consumers, a new model is being demanded in the workplace. People, organizations, and governments need to focus on encouraging experienced professionals and executives, especially women, to start intrapreneurial and entrepreneurial businesses with a strong focus on the Triple Bottom Line—People, Planet, Profit. In this way, we can solve, or at least ameliorate, multiple societal problems simultaneously through the specific social missions of these companies. No doubt the formation of more start-ups focusing on the Triple Bottom Line will have a significant positive effect on the job market, offering a way for all generations to make a living and a difference, and to secure their future and that of the world for generations to come.

The Future of Multigenerational Leadership

Despite the clear trend of Baby Boomers working longer, and some not planning to retire at all, the media, academia, and research firms are still discussing the question, "What will companies do when Baby Boomers step down?" The latest attempt to answer this is found in a report by researchers at Cass Business School at City University London, "After the Baby Boomers: The Next Generation of Leadership."

Their findings are interesting, particularly in the distinctions drawn between the Boomers and Generation X and Y (Millennials), but once again, I have to call into question the premise the entire study is based on—the assumption that Boomers will simply step down from leadership. I believe this premise is false. This is not to say that the younger generations won't be stepping into leadership positions more and more, but that the shift will be gradual, with generations working together. This is a future story for us, but it's being reported as a present story, and doing so only contributes to the disconnect and discord between generations.

Many of the findings of this study are still worth a look, however, even if we dispense with the assumption that we're facing a nice, neat "X in/Boomers out" scenario. The characterization of the X and Millennial generations as being much more ethnically diverse and insistent on work-life balance—for all genders—is just as easily a characterization of business trends as a whole. It's simple: Businesses not actively preparing for and welcoming these trends toward diversity, gender equality, and balance will be left behind by those who are. This is the *real* story of the marketplace now and in the future.

The *real* story is rapidly becoming a happening, but not because these trends are growing as Baby Boomers leave. On the contrary, these trends are growing as Boomers incorporate them into their own core values. Even those of us post-50 who once took part in the now-outdated definitions of success— making money, reaching the executive suite or corner office, achieving, achieving, achieving—have long realized that this kind of success is empty on its own.

Those few Baby Boomers who were still pursuing the "success at all costs" methodology are now facing a future where work-life balance is not a luxury but a necessity.

In other words, no matter how we get there, and no matter what generation we are in, diversity and work-life balance are the keys to futures that work for all of us. Whether we want that balance because we're starting a family or because we want time to visit our established families, the outcome is the same logistically. Work locations and hours must be increasingly flexible for everyone, without penalizing anyone for taking advantage of this flexibility.

The multigenerational businesses that will thrive will have Baby Boomers mentoring the upcoming generations and will provide a clear path for employees who wish to work less, but not retire, to move more and more into consulting and specialized niches. Boomers will need to develop their own succession plan, as well and clarify their what's-next game plan as they begin transitioning, whenever and however that looks (semi-retirement, full retirement, never retirement, encore careers, etc.).

The future is not a zero-sum game or one in which one generation has to lose while the other wins. When we look closely at what all generations want as employees, entrepreneurs, and leaders, we can see that behind the differences are the same aspirational visions and sustainable solutions.

What's interesting is that for all the media hype pitting the generations against one another, more and more members of all generations—X, Millennials, early and late Boomers, and Matures—are becoming more vocal about putting aside the generational stereotypes and looking at the common ground.

The question then becomes not whether these generations will work well together but how, and what changes we are likely to see in the future of business as a result of the changing, more age-diverse face of tomorrow's workforce, from professionals to executives to the growing number of entrepreneurs. What aspirational future story will we create together?

A recent panel called "Don't Generalize My Generation," sponsored by Deutsch NY, raised many interesting answers to this question on topics ranging from work styles to telecommuting. Here I'd like to focus on one area that I think has important implications for all aspects of how—and why—we do business: leadership.

The traditional business model is hierarchical and, at its extreme, this top-down model has meant that those lower in the hierarchy simply "follow orders" based on what the leadership passes down. We all know that this has been changing for decades. The hierarchy is still the most common structure, but more and more businesses recognize the need to cultivate a shared vision, a sense of the big picture and where every person within the organization fits in that picture. I see this as a flattening of the pyramid, not doing away with it entirely.

We are at a remarkable transition point where many among the younger generations expect leadership to be essentially crowd-sourced, a concept that at first blush might seem foreign to their older colleagues. But is it?

It is important that all generations have a shared vision. As Boomers age, the need to focus on what really matters most to them becomes increasingly important. Ultimately, for all generations, true leadership is the vision itself, a purpose that everyone can feel genuinely invested in—not only those working toward that vision as a part of the business but also those the businesses serve. It's a story we co-create and step into together. The trend I'm seeing is from businesses being client-centric, to employee-centric, to *human*-centric, focusing on the humanity of everyone the business touches.

Businesses led by a strong shared story do not rely on holding on for dear life to the same people as leaders, or the same type of people who have always led in our past stories. Story-led businesses can weather changes that result from retirement, job-sharing arrangements, people transitioning from full time to part time, and similar changes in the fluidity of how people manage their careers and their own transitions (be they related to aging, starting a family, or simply wanting to pursue multiple intersecting paths to self-actualization and professional fulfillment).

This fluidity is only going to increase in the future, and it has as much to do with the changing priorities of the older generation as it does with the new expectations and preferences of the younger—and every age and stage in between.

The future story of leadership is not only multigenerational, it is collaborative and, above all, visionary. Those who recognize and nourish this trend, as well as the visionary purpose within all of us, will not only survive but also thrive with their roots in generational common ground.

The Age-Friendly Workplace

Any good story has to include a well-developed setting, and our new story for the future is no different. The term "age-friendly" refers not only to environments and technology that are tailored to the aging population, but also to those that meet the needs of multiple people at all ages and stages of life. One of the key reasons for us to have intergenerational conversations is to determine where our needs and desires intersect and to develop ideas that will meet those needs and desires for as many people as possible.

Some of the most compelling age-friendly ideas for the workplace fall under the umbrella of flexible work arrangements. Long thought of as a concept that caters primarily to women with children, flex work is increasingly being recognized as an ideal way to also serve the needs of those who wish to work beyond retirement age. Not only that, but new research from Catalyst shows that the only companies able to consistently attract and retain top talent, regardless of gender, age, or life stage, are those offering some form of flexible work arrangements.

Further, the research shows that the costs of implementing such a program are offset by savings in operational costs—by more than $10,000 a year per person telecommuting part time.

Telecommuting has become synonymous with flexible work arrangements in many minds, but the former term encompasses many possibilities. Even companies with hourly employees whose work must be done onsite, such as manufacturing work, can benefit employees—and their own bottom line—with various flex options:

- Compressed schedules
- Flexible start and end times
- Job sharing and/or shift trading
- Voluntary overtime (those who want the extra money can work the overtime, and those who don't aren't compelled to)
- Employee-designed schedules

- Sabbatical programs
- Unpaid time off
- Half-day options
- Assignment variety based on availability and skill, not seniority
- Flexible space onsite for employees to use to meet in support groups (such as for people caring for elderly parents, working parents, etc.) or for personal computer use during breaks on long shifts.

What works best—for company and employee—depends on many factors. People have different work styles and preferences, and some tasks are best accomplished in particular ways or at particular times and locations.

Collaboration between the business and employees is key to uncovering what is most important to everyone and why and to determine how employee needs and those of the company can both be met. A regular process for review is essential to adjust what isn't working as well as to meet the changing needs of the organization, its talent, and its customers.

Ultimately, "Continuous Improvement" is about focusing on results and outputs rather than on micromanaging people. The belief that the latter is necessary to the former is contrary to the data. After voluntarily leaving my corporate perch in the late 1980s, I was blessed to synchronistically find myself studying with and under the tutelage of my deeply admired teacher, mentor, and friend, Dr. W. Edwards Deming. He encouraged me to take an even bigger systems' view to identify which outliers or special causes in any process might be producing defects in the outputs or derailing the process, as well as identifying those excelling in producing outputs and innovation within Six Sigma of perfection. ("Six Sigma" is lots of things depending on how it is applied, but in short it is a metric, as well as a rigorous and disciplined methodology, that aids in quality improvement and overall quality management.)

There is an old Chinese saying that I'll paraphrase: "When the fish stinks, it stinks from the top!" Deming knew this saying to be true, and he went on to prove it to be so in his many real-time international and national corporate client stories, in his Continuous Improvement studies, and so much more detailed in his many notable books, articles, and talks. In his own words (that say it all), "The worker is not the problem. The problem is at the top! Management!" Dr. Deming expanded this statement even further by adding, "95% of all the problems and failures in business are system failures; it has nothing to do with the individual manager or worker and only 5% are people driven." He ardently believed that 95 percent of these same problems in business are caused by management because they create and are responsible to manage the system. Only the leader can change the system. So if the workers or employees screw up, it's most certainly not their fault! Sadly, Deming was also spot-on when he declared, "A poor system will win every time over a good employee."

The most important thing I learned from Deming is his theory that system correction must come from the top down (vs. blaming workers) if its to make a difference, a sustainable lasting improvement. In fact, he stated in his book *Out of the Crisis* that the most important strategic action to take is to continuously improve the system and its processes to realize sustainable, ongoing process improvement and high-quality results.

I was very fortunate to study with and be mentored by Dr. Deming, especially since by the time I met him he was firmly committed to transformation and the importance of his lifelong body of work codified by his later life's *System of Profound Knowledge*, (SoPK). This system is an incredibly effective theory of management, applicable no matter the size of an organization or its mission. That is, if you or your organization seek to transform and create a thriving organization with win-win as your foundational objective, follow Deming's system of knowledge model.

Dr. Deming's legacy is saved for eternity within the W. Edwards Deming Institute he founded in 1993. In the institute's own descriptive mission statement, "The Deming Institute is bringing the teachings of Dr. W. Edwards Deming to a new generation, for a rapidly evolving new world. We believe in inspiring individuals and organizations to make a difference, think differently, ask better questions and seek new knowledge."

He believed and demonstrated in his world-famous "Red Bead Experiment" (an exercise wherein executives play both the part of the worker and management), the truism that intrinsic rewards achieve far greater motivation, innovation, and ever-increasing quality, productivity, and outputs. Yes, we are in more disruptive times now, and rapid response to change demands innovation and creativity, which seems the antithesis of Deming's insistence to reduce variability in our systems and processes. To be sure, he never suggested that innovative outliers should be thwarted; rather, he encouraged innovation with continuous quality improvement (CQI) built in to the very underpinnings of every system and process. Indeed, Deming never suggested that a system is foolproof. Quite the opposite, he took the view that any existing system is satisfactory for accomplishing the work of today, but he also insisted that we must constantly improve our systems and processes to prepare to address the problems of tomorrow as well as the problems of today. I had the grand pleasure of reading his drafts for his *Out of the Crisis*, which is a Total Quality Management bible for the rest of us. If Deming's fourteen points are followed to a tee, then long-term success is ensured.

Survival is optional. No one has to change.

~Dr. W. Edwards Deming, P.h.D

Dr. Deming's over two hundred published writings, including papers, articles and books, are not a quick read, nor for the dilettante. A good starting point is to avail yourself of the many resources available through The W. Edwards Deming Institute online (www.Deming.org).

If Deming were alive today, he'd be a raving fan of age-friendly workplaces.

We can all work toward creating age-friendly workplaces by bringing these ideas, and the facts behind them, to the attention of our employers, especially if we wish or need to stay until we transition into retirement, a new career, or entre-preneurship. If you own or manage a business or organization, you are in a perfect position for guiding your employees to create an age-friendly workplace together.

As more and more employers recognize the need to capitalize on their experienced workforce in order to retain them, we should see an increasing emphasis on flexible work arrangements—part-time work, consulting, and job sharing, just to name a few. This, in turn, will provide more visible options for Baby Boomers to consider beyond the false dichotomy of retiring or not retiring.

Forward-thinking companies have already begun this shift, but far too many are not looking past their own noses to prepare for the coming wave of Baby Boomers making pivotal choices about how to design their lives and their stories around work. For many businesses, the planning for a changing workforce won't happen until the sheer numbers of Boomers on the precipice of leaving reach a critical mass, or until multiple generations start working together to make these changes happen. Waiting is a huge mistake for these businesses, of course, yet this lack of foresight does not have to extend to the rest of us.

We all have the opportunity, no matter our age or stage, to design our futures starting today, to create an aspirational future story for our work lives. You don't have to wait for your company to provide options for you. Now is the time to develop your own game plan, to think BIG about the next stage of your life, and to then create your own options to make that big vision happen.

This manifestation may mean going to your employer and laying out your plans and what you need from them to make those plans happen in ways that are advantageous for both of you. Or this may mean laying out a succession and exit strategy that takes you into your own business, your chance to combine passion, profit, and purpose, to make a living and a difference while enjoying more flexibility to work where and when you want.

Parents of young children and 70-year-olds alike can find work or create businesses that are flexible in hours and location (among myriad other factors), to work with their realities and their desire to focus on what matters most. Organizations that do not recognize the need to customize the work world for every employee will find that their employees will do it themselves, especially in midlife and beyond. These companies will not only lose the experience and wisdom of their post-50 staff, teams, and leaders, but they are likely to lose money to many of them as former employees become entrepreneurial competition.

Boomerpreneurs and Solopreneurs

A significant number of the many people who plan to continue working past retirement age are or will be entrepreneurs. This fact is part of the present story for Boomers, and all signs point to it being integral to the future Boomer story. According to the Kauffman Foundation, people ages 55 to 64 consistently start more new businesses than those in any other age group, and this reality has been true for about a decade. We also know from this foundation that people over 55 are the most likely to be successful with their business start-ups. The Sloan Center on Aging & Work estimates that about 38 percent of small business owners (including solo companies) are age 60 or older.

Even more interesting is that in a recent Civic Ventures survey of 45- to 70-year-olds, about 25 percent indicated an interest in being entrepreneurs, and more than half of them wanted their venture to address a social issue.

The years ahead may be the era of the Boomerpreneur and solopreneur, as we collectively reinvent work after 40 and turn stereotypes about aging and retirement on their head, re-storying what it means to live and work at any age. Not only will more and more people age 40 and beyond be looking to start or grow their own businesses, or continue leading their organizations, they will also represent the largest market segment for these businesses, which is one of the reasons it makes so much sense to start off thinking about solutions for your own needs and problems. Necessity may be the mother of invention, but in the twenty-first century, the grandmother of invention is reinvention—of yourself, your future, your business, your world, and your story.

In fact, the 40-plus market is perfect for a new encore entrepreneurial start-up, the opportunity to change ageism into age-friendly while making a profit. Boomer women are at the forefront of this movement. An increasing number of women are rising to executive and board positions (though still not even close to the number of men). According to the National Association of Women Business Owners, more women are running successful businesses, generating $1.3 trillion in annual sales and showing net increases in employment, growth that can only be matched by large publicly traded corporations. With this increasing rise in women's power, there has been a backlash in American society and in the workplace, and older women bear the brunt of it. Women of all ages witness repeated cycles of ageism and related firings under the guise of "poor performance" that have nothing to do with measurable performance and everything to do with measurable age. Women, and men too, see their older colleagues being pushed aside, diminished, and ostracized by frightened colleagues who fear they might catch the firing bug if they stay connected. Rather than staying in repressive, stultifying positions with a silver ceiling looming and poor performance reviews on the horizon as they head toward 50 and beyond, regardless of actual performance, women are standing in their own shoes and starting their own businesses, particularly as solopreneurs. And many of them are savvy enough to recognize the most important market out there: women just like them.

Starting or Reinventing a Business after 40

Whether you are thinking about starting a business or are already running your own company, the next steps are similar. Even those already in business must frequently reassess how their business is doing, and not just financially. You might be considering how to add more meaning to your business and work life, how to combine what you are already doing with ways to make a bigger difference in the world.

Regardless of your situation, your first step is to consider what kind of business you want to create, evolve, or reinvent. The new story for your business needs an outline. Scan and ponder the ten questions that follow. You can consider these questions more fully when you take time to focus on the Reflections at the end of this chapter.

1. Do you want to continue in your current field or try something new? If new, is it related to your existing

skill set or industry, or will you need further education and training before you can open your doors? If in your current field, are you in love with what you do, or are you choosing this field because it's familiar? Choose something that you are genuinely, passionately interested in, that you are already drawn to read about, talk about, and learn about at every opportunity. If you are planning to reinvent an existing business, you need to go beyond what you've done in the past—beyond good service to extraordinary service, beyond meeting expectations to exceeding them and offering a lot more value-added services or products. How does this look in terms of what you could offer, and how does that compare to what you do already?

2. How will your business address what matters most to you? In what ways do you want your business to also address what matters most to your family, your community, the world? Will it meet the Triple Bottom Line: People, Planet, Profit? Where do your talents and passions intersect with what the world needs now and what it will need in the future?

3. Do you want to sell products, provide services, consult, or some combination?

4. Do you want to go totally virtual with your business or a combination? Which option suits your lifestyle choices?

5. Do you want to be a solopreneur or do you want to be an employer?

6. If starting a new business, what kind of time and

money are you willing and able to invest in the first three years (the average lag time between starting a business and breaking even)? If reinventing your business, what time and money are you willing and able to invest to revitalize and revamp what you're already doing?

7. What is the income potential for your business? Will it be enough to meet your needs? Will it be enough to meet your desires? Make an appointment with an accountant and business growth expert who has experience with entrepreneurs to get a realistic assessment of your business costs and potential.

8. What kind of competition is out there? How are they doing, particularly since the recession? How will you do things differently to stand out, avoid the competition's mistakes, and capitalize on trends so that you are ahead of change?

9. What does the day-to-day operation look like to you realistically? What do you want the day-to-day operation to look like?

   - Consider how lifestyle-compatible your business is. If you live near the top of a mountain, a business that requires a lot of in-person contact or travel will be tricky without easy and affordable transportation. If you need regular human interaction, don't create a business model that chains you to your computer all day. If you want to sustain your business indefinitely, doing the work you love into your nineties or beyond, design your business to weather any physical changes you might encounter down the road. Consider how much freedom and flexibility you want—to travel, spend time with family and friends, do volunteer work, or just relax whenever you need to.

- Consider what everyday tasks you enjoy, which ones you find mundane but doable, and which ones you loathe. Will you have a balance? Will you be able to delegate the latter? Or will the day-to-day requirements of your business idea likely damper the passion you have for the business? Will you have enough variety or enough routine to suit your personality, needs, and preferences?

10. How tech savvy are you now, and how tech savvy will you need to be to run your business successfully? What technology is required for the business itself? What technology is required for marketing, accounting, sales, distribution, etc.? What new technologies can keep your business on the edge of change? Even the most experienced, savvy professionals will need to be on a continuous technological learning curve to keep up with the changing marketplace. If you don't have the interest or time to learn new technology, can you afford to get technical help as needed? If you are planning a business that you can run for the next thirty, forty, or fifty years, consider now what technology can enable you to do that, including what you would need to keep your business running virtually.

The future of business, and of our world, lies in the hands of those who are taking steps right now to reimagine the marketplace, the workplace, and the small business in ways that intersect with where we are headed as well as where we want to head globally—sustainability, cooperative business models, flexibility in our work and our lives, and the ability to pursue what is meaningful to us in everything we do, at every age.

Time Is Money

At this point, you may know that you want to start a business but still feel unsure about exactly what kind of business. You may only vaguely know that you want to do something purposeful, but you aren't sure if this means volunteering, work, or some combination, or what exactly you would be doing.

If you have not yet decided on what you want to do, consider the opportunities inherent in our most precious resource—time.

For all the timesaving technology we gain each year, we somehow seem to have less and less time available to us. Busy working parents don't have as much time to volunteer in schools or spend as much time with their children as they'd like. Even kids don't have as much time for free play with all their activities, sports, and school-related commitments. In an increasingly urban society, some kids have the time for free play but no safe spaces to do so, and their parents don't have time to take them to safe spaces.

Many areas of traditional volunteer work, such as visiting with the sick and infirm, feeding the homeless, helping to care for animals in shelters, and so forth, are lacking in volunteers because people simply do not have the time.

One answer, of course, is to simply step up and be a volunteer. But consider looking at this from a different perspective. How can you or your business save people time in ways that specifically allow them to have more meaningful time? With their children? Their parents? Volunteering themselves? In essence, ask what plot holes there are in the present story of your community? Where are the gaps that need attention? How can you fill them and give new direction not only to the story of others but also your own?

If you run (or plan to run) a business with employees, designing flexible work schedules could be a part of how you set up your workforce. Using job sharing, flexible hours, work-at-home days, and so forth will enable your employees to balance their lives by being able to choose the options that work best for them. Or your business could be the meaningful work that you (with or without employees) want the time to do.

If you are still with a company, planning your own eventual exit, now is the time to research and develop alternate preferred scenarios that could serve you, your colleagues, and the business, such as a consultant relationship or part-time substitute situation that enables everyone to take "meaning days," along with the traditional vacation time and sick time.

Any business that brings extended families and communities together to help one another out and save time is bound to hit a ready market. What if busy parents only worried about cooking dinner once or twice a week? How about a service that brings young kids to meet with parents over lunch near or at their work?

How about a program for companies to buy into that sends groups of employees to volunteer with their families in the name of the company?

The possibilities are endless—as are the potential profits—when you consider what is truly meaningful to you and to others. Contrary to the trope about the later years of life, time really is on our side.

Grannypreneurs

Along the same lines as focusing on providing ways for others to strengthen relationships, another avenue to consider is accommodating the changing needs of grandparents. When thinking about the needs of Baby Boomers and Matures, whether as members of these groups or as those who serve them (or both!), products and services for children may not even be on our radar. Yet grandparents and even later-life parents are spending more time and money on children than ever before.

A recent MetLife survey found that grandparents are spending an average of $8,661 annually on grandchildren, a number likely to increase as younger Boomers become grandparents. Consider this number in light of the Boomer Values Realignment Survey that found "a big shift from consumerism to relationships" in Boomer focus.

If you already run a business, targeting your existing products and services to Baby Boomers and Matures is only part of the picture. Transcending the status quo by focusing on ways to help grandparents spend more quality time strengthening their relationships with their grandchildren and children has visionary potential for you and for the people you serve.

If you are a grandparent and an entrepreneur (or just thinking about starting your own business), this trend provides you with an opportunity to look at your own needs and desires and align them with what others in your tribe are seeking.

UK research supporting the positive trajectory for Boomerpreneurs, and most definitely grannypreneurs (which most likely reflects U.S. study results as well), has revealed that modernday "grand-trepreneurs" are the over-sixties real boomerang generation. A quarter of these retirement-age adults working into later life run their own business, with 21 percent opening their doors while in their sixties. The conclusion drawn by the reporter is that these over-60 entrepreneurs show that there is a trend to "unretire" or to never retire.

Just as Baby Boomers are changing the way we all age, they are likely to redefine the role grandparents have played in the past. By anticipating the needs of this reimagining— especially by drawing on your own needs and desires for the present and future—you can create a sustainable business and lifestyle in which what matters most to you in life is integral to making a living. Grannypreneurs just might be the sleeper story of the future!

Boomerpreneurs and Technology

One of the most pervasive myths about Baby Boomers is that we are technology Luddites. As with any generational stereotype, there are certainly individuals that fit this bill, but as a whole, Boomers are the fastest-growing group of technology users, not to mention the generation that invented much of the technology that is ubiquitous today. In fact, many of the successful post-50 start-ups are in fact tech start-ups. The true present story of Boomers and tech is very different from the mythical present.

The digital performance marketing company iProspect published a study titled "The Ageless Internet: From Silver Surfers to Golden Geeks," which reveals that confidence in technology and Internet usage is as high in the over-50s as it is among the 30 to 49 demographic. Importantly, the findings show that the older group is just as digitally savvy as younger generations. To underscore their conclusion that the digital age divide is a myth, they found a full 80 percent of 50- to 59-year-olds believe their age is no barrier to using the Internet, and they expect to use it more in the future. Mind-blowing is that this percentage rises to 88 percent of 60- to 69-year-olds, and to as many as 92 percent of those age 70 or more.

When it comes to the social edge, 28 million 50-plussers already subscribe to Facebook. The Forrester Research study finds that the Boomer demographic buys twice as much online as younger adults.

Deloitte published a report that concludes that older consumers are likely to continue working, accumulate an ever-greater share of global wealth and become increasingly interested in technology. Ben Perkins, who is head of consumer business research at this Big Four accountancy firm, sees this as an important market for future growth. According to Deloitte's report, smartphone ownership among the over-55ers was predicted to double by 2014. With all the large-screen smartphones now on the market, there is no cap in sight on this explosive growth curve.

I think Apple's retail service is darn good, although the lines can be tough to maneuver. Yet I've often wondered why Apple doesn't segment its service by training older staff Geniuses and sales staff to serve older customers. Tesco, the UK's largest retailer, is doing just that to sell mobile technology. Perkins at Deloitte raves about this new model: "Basically there's somebody of the same generation who understands the subtleties and differences between what a twenty-five-year-old and what a fifty-five-year-old may be looking for in a mobile device."

But for many of us, technology is a means to an end more than an end in itself. If we are thinking about starting or reinventing a business, technology plays a minimal role—if any role at all—in deciding what kind of business we want to create or transform. If anything, technology comes in at the later stages, when we try to conform the latest advances to our existing ideas. Backing into technology further into the process can be frustrating when we have to jury rig the tech to suit our business model, especially if we are also still learning how to use it in the first place.

Seth Godin discussed an aspect of this after-the-fact insertion of technology in a blog post, giving examples of changes in technology that have required more than just slight adjustments in how businesses are run: mail to email; books to e-books; Visa to PayPal; direct mail to permission marketing, and so on. As he points out: "The question that gets asked about technology, the one that is almost always precisely the wrong question is, 'How does this advance help our business?' The correct question is, 'How does this advance undermine our business model and require us/enable us to build a new one?'"

Not only must we be lifelong learners of technological advances, but we also must be prepared to look at all the new possibilities for our businesses and continuously reinvent to take advantage of them. Adapting the technology to our old methods and perspectives simply won't work long term. We are the ones who must adapt.

Ask yourself: What possibilities in the latest technology inspire an entrepreneurial reinvention—or a brand-new business?

The Social Edge

Of course, it also makes sense to take a look at how you can creatively use the technology you're already familiar with, such as social media, which Baby Boomers are using with rapidly increasing frequency in their personal and professional lives. Whether you're thinking of recareering or starting a business, or you just want to rev up your existing career or business, recent trends point to a way post-40 women especially can capitalize on their strengths.

Online recruiter Jobvite has reported that 94 percent of recruiters use or plan to use social media to find candidates. Although the company will obviously have a bias in its numbers because it makes social media recruiting software, even being conservative and lowering this percentage shows a distinct trend.

Couple this with the Hiscox studies showing that female entrepreneurs are experiencing a more rapid rate of growth than male entrepreneurs and that one reason for this growth is women's use of social media in all aspects of their businesses, not just for hiring.

Fast Company recently highlighted stories of women and men using social media to launch new careers or businesses, including the following:

- Kay Roseland, who was laid off in her sixties, decided to get certifications in social media and start a blog. Then through social media contact, followed by face-to-face contact, she ended up landing a job blogging for Infor.com.

- At 50, Gail Dosik went from the fashion industry to culinary school, then started her own Manhattan bakery, building word of mouth through social media and email.

- Attorney Diane Danielson recareered into marketing in her forties, jumping into an on-the-job crash course in social media and web-based marketing, ultimately landing a job when she wasn't even looking for one simply through her online presence.

For women, being social can mean big business, especially for those in midlife and beyond. One of the most persistent stereotypes about Baby Boomers and Matures is that they are unwilling to learn new things and are not on top of the latest technology. The stats show otherwise (see studies by the Kauffman Foundation and Northwestern's Kellogg School of Management mentioned above), but public perception often lags behind reality. One of the best ways to change the stereotype, to change the story, is to be a visible example of its opposite.

On top of this lagging, out-of-date public perception, we are at a critical point coming out of the Great Recession during a time of unprecedented technology and increasing numbers of people putting their money where their values are. This groundswell of value-based action means we are in a position to shape what business looks like going forward, including using our businesses and careers to build genuine connections with others, combine our values with our business practices, and make a profit in innovative, meaningful ways. Social media is also all about storytelling, a place to share the story you are creating for yourself and to co-create stories for the future of the marketplace and the global community.

All of these potential opportunities for a new story capitalize on the current strengths of many women and of social media. Right now, you are in a unique position to redefine business, not only for yourself but also for generations to come, by combining the two.

Perhaps the examples above or other success stories are exactly the path you want to take, or perhaps you will simply follow your own natural path in building relationships and using social media in ways that are comfortable for you.

Whatever you do, from investing in your social media education or business practices to simply increasing or innovating within your existing social media use, remember that online and off, showing up and having presence are essential components to opening yourself up for opportunities, sometimes when you least expect them.

Today and into the future, building relationships is building your business, even if—especially if—that business is you.

The Future of Podcasting

The fast-growing podcasting trend allows all of us to meet our tribe, our audience(s), where they are. Edison Research recently reported that a stunning 39 million Americans have listened to a podcast in a typical month. But clearly this is only a bellwether of what's to come. If we step back to look at why this current trend is growing, it makes total sense. Podcasting is a medium that provides freedom to connect wherever you are (even on technology as small as portable smartphones), and whenever it suits the listener (since it's solely audio content, it is available around the clock). Pretty soon it will be a no-brainer to dial up a podcast, even in our cars. Before we get too excited, there is a big BUT. Women are underrepresented in podcaster land. What an opportunity for we women who love to share our stories, and converse with our peeps!

Ageless Technology

There's one area of technology that often flies under the radar when we're talking about Baby Boomers and tech, yet the impact is profound, as well as demonstrating how technology with purposes specific to this demographic can serve all ages.

Few people think of Bluetooth earpieces or e-readers like Kindle as being technology designed for our needs as we age, yet some earpieces can filter out background noise and boost our ability to hear clearly, particularly in crowds, and e-readers can be adjusted in multiple ways to make the type easier to read for all vision types.

Similarly, technology for fitness and health, financial management, travel planning, and more are advancements useful across generations. Yet they all hit a sweet spot, most notably with the post-50 generations who have a heightened interest in this technology with each passing year.

These products are so ordinary that it's easy to overlook them when we're thinking in terms of our own use of technology as well as in terms of making our products and services friendlier to the enormous Boomer market.

The key is not to look at technology that is only for 50-plussers. This mind-set stems from an Othering of people over a "certain age" that is a relic of our past. Instead, we should be looking at creating and buying technology that is multifunctional and user-friendly so that it ages with us, adapting to our needs over a lifetime.

The future of technology is truly Ageless.

Your Visionary Business

All visionaries are Ageless, and we all have a visionary voice inside us. That voice can guide us toward making a difference in the world while simultaneously achieving sustainable, meaningful success in our lives and work.

Many of you are no doubt aware of this voice. Maybe you've had to reawaken it at various times in your life—most of us have to do this—but you know it's there.

Some of you, on the other hand, might not see yourself as ever being a visionary. Visionaries are other people, not you.

You have ideas, but you don't see them as earth-shattering. You want sustainable, meaningful success, sure, but nothing you're planning will transform the world.

And that's okay. Your definition of success, of what matters most to you, is yours and yours alone. But if at any point in your life you've felt that you were meant for more, that there's a bigger purpose inside you yet to be realized, then you are selling yourself—and the world—short by not uncovering that purpose, by not doing what you can to awaken your visionary voice and allow it to narrate your future.

This acknowledgement is crucial if your reasons for not doing so are that you think it's too late for you, or that you are not smart enough, rich enough, confident enough, creative enough…that you are simply not enough to lead change.

It is never too late to be a visionary. On the contrary, many of us can't be true visionaries until we have the experience, wisdom, and willingness to focus only on what matters— qualities that tend to ripen with age.

You don't have to wait until you feel you are enough. Awaken the visionary voice inside, and you will find that your doubts become insignificant in light of a vision you will be driven to pursue, with passion, purpose, and, yes, even profit. I have found that awakening our Inner Visionary requires profound inner work along with parallel outer due diligence. Please be sure not to shortcut this endeavor, or you surely will end up going in circles or aborting your efforts. You may even want to proceed with this discovery process under the expert and experienced tutelage of a trained professional who has both the know-how and knowledge of the psyche, as well as the real-world knowledge of careers and business to guide you to find where your gifts intersect with what the world needs now.

And that brings me back to those of you who do not feel driven to uncover your larger Soul's purpose, to discover how your personal and professional success can run parallel to making a difference in the world.

Consider this: The more turmoil our world undergoes— economic, environmental, social—the more everyday people choose to spend their money on products and services that in some way go toward healing our Earth. In other words, when given a choice between two companies with essentially the same offering, consumers are increasingly choosing the one that goes that extra step toward making a difference in the world.

Think about where this trend is going. People and businesses that find a way to combine a larger visionary purpose with their business model will be the most profitable. More people and businesses will follow their lead until visionary business practices will become the norm. Not riding this trend now not only means missing out on a larger market, more money, and greater impact—it could make your ideas and your business ultimately obsolete. »

CHAPTER 2 ~ *Reflections*

The questions and exercises below are to help you find your distinct path to rocking your revenues in the Longevity Economy. Turn to page vii for more about the Gray is the New Green Reflections.

1. What story are you in right now with your work? Where do you see that story going in the future? What other preferred future scenarios are possible for you? Which has the best possible outcome? Which story do you want to be living and working in the next year or two? Once you have your alternative futures laid out, you can focus on and manifest the one you most want.

2. What does "retirement" mean to you? Are you planning to retire or partially retire at any age? Are your plans part of an old story, one you are living because you are expected to? What changes would you make to workplaces and the ways businesses are run in order to co-create a new story about working past 65 or 70?

3. How does your existing business or business idea root itself in your values? What are you doing to build and deepen genuine relationships, professionally and personally?

4. What opportunities do you have for multigenerational conversations in the workplace? What can you do to change these conversations, to make them collaborative and based on finding common-ground solutions that work for all ages and stages?

5. What are the ideal elements of a workplace that would serve you now and into the foreseeable future? In other words, what does the new work story look like for you? What can you do to start making these changes? Do they all point to starting your own business, as an entrepreneur or solopreneur?

6. What aspects of technology are ideal for you and/or your business? What aspects are more difficult to work with? What would technology without these difficulties look like? Which of these difficulties reflect potential problems with your current ways of doing things, personally and professionally? Could you change your processes or systems in ways that alleviate these difficulties?

7. Determining the new story for your business takes some deep digging to discover what kind of business you want to create, evolve or reinvent. Consider re-exploring the questions on pages 81-84.

Chapter 3

STAYING IN SYNC WITH THE PEOPLE WHO KEEP YOU IN BUSINESS

In times of renaissance, when the landscape of future history stands vast and open before us, we have a rare opportunity to put our imagination to work reinventing ourselves and our civilization.

~ Jean Houston, Author

Rewriting Our Life Story

Life doesn't end after 40! We must trash that tired, old story and write ourselves an entirely new one—one that reinvents our futures in ways that make the post-midlife era just a transition into reimagined ways of doing and being, rather than a time of retiring and waiting to expire.

Let's engage the middle-age-and-up mindset in a way that captures the momentum of this forward-thinking progress. It's more than perception—it's an evolutionary change in the business community that seeks to engage the work community and transcend itself into the entire Ageless population.

Studies show that 84 percent of women feel misunderstood by marketers who are out of touch with what real women want and need, how they see themselves, and how they want to see themselves. Women still want products and therapies that enhance our beauty or slow the aging process, but on their own they are not enough. We also want to feel beautiful and Ageless inside and out. Marketers, and society as a whole, need to understand that we no longer wish to be told that aging is something we need to be against. Agelessness is about embracing and enhancing who we are, not blindly following an outdated standard of who we should be.

Businesses that embark upon a quest to transform the conversation about aging will take advantage of what employees have to offer in mid- and later life. So how do we begin? Business leaders are in the best position to guide this conversation and, even more, to go beyond lip service and act. How will you change your business, your community, your country to incorporate an active aging workforce, to harness the wisdom and experience of the people who just might be the ones to jump-start our economy and protect our Earth for generations to come?

Solopreneurs and entrepreneurs have a role to play, too. Your businesses have the unique opportunity to come at the 40-plus market from the ground up. How will you help an aging community remain relevant in today's world, and change your community's mindset so that relevance of the older set is less a surprise than a given? How can you target that market, which controls an enormous amount of wealth, in a way that gives them more meaningful time with their loved ones? In a way that makes a difference in their lives, as well as puts a profit in your pocket?

It's apparent that our aging Boomer leadership is forcing a shift in the over-the-hill mind-set, but at what age are we truly over the hill? Does it matter? In her book *Seriously I'm Kidding*, comedian Ellen DeGeneres—herself 58 years young—wrote, "It must be around 40 when you're 'over the hill.' I don't even know what that means and why it's a bad thing. When I go hiking and I get over the hill, that means I'm past the hard part and there's a snack in my future. That's a good thing as far as I'm concerned."

The Silver Screen Is Changing Pop Culture

For years there has been a lack of older female leads in Hollywood—often at the forefront of cultural change. Breaking the mold, 2013 and 2014 were great years for actresses over 40, indications that Hollywood has begun to shift its focus toward producing films by and for the mature majority market. Indeed, older women are breaking the silver screen's once-impregnable silver ceiling. Women over 50 accounted for 80 percent of female Oscar nominees from films released in 2013. This included many of our favorite stars like Judi Dench (then 79) in *Philomena*, Meryl Streep (then 64) in *August: Osage County*, Emma Thompson (then 55) in *Saving Mr. Banks*, Sandra Bullock (then 50) in *Gravity*, and June Squibb (then 84) in *Nebraska*.

The nominees for the 2015 Oscars—films released in 2014—included Meryl Streep (then 66) for *Into the Woods*, Julianne Moore (then 55) for *Still Alice*, and—on the cusp of 50—Laura Dern (then 48) for *Wild* and Patricia Arquette (then 47) for *Boyhood*. The 2016 Oscars saw nominations for

Charlotte Rampling (69) for *45 Years*, Jennifer Jason Leigh (53) for *The Hateful Eight*, Cate Blanchette (46) for *Carol*, and Kate Winslet (40) for *Steve Jobs*. 2016 keeps the meme going with the enormous success of the *Best Exotic Marigold Hotel* and the new release of *The Intern* starring Robert De Niro portraying the new prototypical "senior intern."

This goes to show that though the 1930s and early 1940s were considered Hollywood's "Golden Age," a more literal golden age is happening right now, as so many older actresses are reaching the pinnacles of their professions, thereby inspiring the masses who watch their successes and translate those good vibes into changing the dialogue about aging.

Since this story is already changing on the silver screen, as well as in ads targeting women, among women, and around the kitchen table, it's high time the conversation took place around the boardroom table in companies marketing to women, as well as those who should start serving the 40-plus market of savvy, accomplished, mature women.

Women mean business.
Boomer women mean BIG business.

Ageless Women are strong, multifaceted, unique, and real. They control the largest percentage of purchasing power in this country. Ageless Women are the future. Businesses that do not recognize and respect who we really are, what we want, and how we deserve to be served, will soon be a thing of the past, aged out!

Think about this. Among United States encore entrepreneurs, Baby Boomer women are more prevalent than men.

These powerful, savvy women—most of them social entrepreneurs—are well connected and ready to rock their revenues. Boomers of both genders control $19 trillion—more than 75 percent of U.S. wealth—and they outpace other generations in nearly every buying category. Women control 85 percent of consumer spending, and Boomer women account for 95 percent of the purchase decisions for their households. What's even more, the market is expected to grow by more than 30 percent in the next 20 years.

Those businesses that recognize the new rules of the game will gobble up market share. We risk losing out in that if we ignore the potential of the 40-plus market. Let's wake up to this risk and get on board fast—our ability to monetize going forward will depend on our willingness to serve this enormous force of new Boomer demand in the workplace, the U.S. marketplace, and around the globe.

As for the 50-plus group? It's morphing everything in its path as it moves from an elongated productive midlife into a later and later onset of old old age. This force of older people in the U.S. alone is composed of 106 million people responsible for at least $7.1 trillion in annual economic activity—a figure that is expected to reach well over $13.5 trillion in real terms by 2032. The Longevity Economy isn't just defined by demographics. This term also applies to the total of all economic activity related to serving the needs of the mature audience.

Ever-elongating lifespans, while a joy and relief to anyone who embraces the later years, pose the problem of how to make our money last throughout the entire journey. Clearly, sound financial planning is an enormously important piece of the pie. But that's an ideal-world answer, not necessarily a real-world one, as the U.S. continues its recovery from the Great Recession, and as the costs of caring for relatives (and ourselves) weigh heavily.

As employers, what more can we do? We must enact change within our companies to ensure that those who want to continue bringing in a paycheck past mid-life aren't shuffled aside. Businesses that embrace flexible work schedules—including job-sharing, telecommuting, and shorter workweeks—can help turn our workplaces into age-friendly spaces. Employers and employees alike will benefit from these arrangements, in which those gifted with extra years can use that accumulation of knowledge to benefit our less-experienced colleagues. There's no need or benefit in forcing retirement at a certain age.

Among all generations, diversity and work-life balance are instrumental to a bright future. The businesses that will thrive will be multigenerational, utilizing Baby Boomers to mentor the upcoming generations. They'll clear the way for employees who wish to work less, but not retire. Why do we even have a "retirement age," anyway? We know that people are living longer, healthier, more active lives. So it doesn't make much sense to be thinking about a retirement age for someone who is functionally in her 40s yet with the experience and wisdom of her full 60 years. We may want or need to work less, or to have more flexible working arrangements, but different generations can surely agree that people of all ages need that!

People of any age may wish to never retire, not even at 90 or 100. They may want to keep working, creating, innovating, inspiring, leading. They simply need to make adaptations in these pursuits that take into account the realities of their lives—just as we all need to do at *every* age. How can you help make this truth the norm?

The Triple Bottom Line

Agelessness is no utopian idea. It's actually a pragmatic approach to economic growth, national well-being, investment in the future, and innovation that could save us and our happiness—and even the planet. If your business is not already serving or planning to serve the 40-plus market, you are missing out financially. Even more, you're missing out on the chance to align what matters with the Boomer audience, which is consciously choosing companies that are making a difference as well as a profit. The future belongs to those who are starting these transformations now.

So now that the new business dynamic has shifted from a time-tested, product-centered one to a pragmatic, employee and customer-centered one, you'll need to help your business to tap into this trend. Focus on shifting your focus—from value to values, from the bottom line to the Triple Bottom Line: People, Planet, Profit. This means that you'll reap the most rewards by melding a larger visionary purpose into your business model. More people and businesses will follow your lead until visionary business practices become the norm. Ride this trend now to take full advantage of a larger market, more money, and greater impact. Ignore it, and you risk making your ideas and your business ultimately obsolete. So start thinking—how can you market your current business or a new venture toward the aging population in a mutually beneficial way?

The more start-ups that launch using the Triple Bottom Line platform, the bigger the boost to the job market. In this way, all generations will have a chance to make both a living and a difference, securing their future and that of generations to come.

You may not be in the right life stage right now for creating or reinvigorating your own business, changing or reinventing your career, transforming your organization. But there's no time like the present for doing the prep work that will enable you to make that leap with confidence when you're ready.

Business Focus: Building Ageless Workplaces

Businesses that don't embrace older employees risk losing valuable resources as the 40-plus set stands in their own shoes and starts their own businesses, particularly as solopreneurs. And many of them are savvy enough to recognize the most important market out there: women just like them. To build an Ageless workplace, visionary employers must mull over how to best retain their most skilled workers.

- What if organizations, academia, families, and local and national government start looking at the needs and wants of society on an individual basis rather than lumping us by age?

- What if flexible work arrangements become the norm— for whoever wants or needs them?

- What if lifelong learning is implemented and sponsored in every nook and cranny of society—for all ages?

- What if we seek ways for those with health and disability issues (their own or their families') to adapt their lives without worry, without having to give up on their life goals, allowing them to continue giving back to society through their work, their creations, their leadership?

Some of the most compelling age-friendly ideas for the workplace fall under the umbrella of flexible work arrangements. Long thought of as a concept that caters primarily to women with children, flex work is increasingly being recognized as an ideal way to also serve the needs of those who wish to work beyond retirement age. Not only that, but research shows that the only companies able to consistently attract and retain top talent, regardless of gender, age, or life stage, are those offering some form of flexible work arrangements.

According to a new study by University of Minnesota sociologists, employees who can reduce their work-family conflict will be happier and healthier—and that's a big check in the win column for the companies that employ them, in terms of productivity and loyalty. The study, "Changing Work and Work-Family Conflict: Evidence from the Work, Family, and Health Network," used a sample of about 700 from the IT department of a Fortune 500 company, giving half more control over where and when they worked as well as more supervisor support for this change. Supervisor support is key—employees can be hesitant to change things up if they know their supervisors aren't on board. The other half, the control group, worked under the company's normal conditions. The researchers found that the employees who were allowed to alter their work environments reported less work-family conflict. They said they had enough time for their families and a better sense of control over their work schedules.

Telecommuting is one of the most common types of flexible work arrangement, but that's not possible for all companies. When work must be done onsite, employees can still benefit with various other flex options:

- Compressed schedules

- Flexible start and end times

- Job sharing and/or shift trading

- Voluntary overtime

- Employee-designed schedules

- Sabbatical programs

- Unpaid time off

- Half-day options

- Assignment variety based on availability and skill, not seniority

- Flexible space onsite for employees to use to meet in support groups or for personal computer use during breaks on long shifts.

Business Focus:
Eliminate The Generational Divide

Studies show that younger generations can accelerate their careers by learning from the hands-on mentorship, wisdom, and experience of older colleagues. Unfortunately, studies also show that ageism is a barrier to this kind of collaborative learning. A study by the Association for Talent Development found not only that all generations stereotype one another, but also that this stereotyping leads to unaddressed tension and conflict that saps productivity by as much as 12 percent!

Be sure that your employees know that the future is not a win/lose proposition among different generations pitted against each other. We all want the same thing—for productive employees of any age to have the right and ability to work side by side. When we look closely at what all generations want as employees, entrepreneurs, and leaders, we can see that behind the differences are the same aspirational visions and sustainable solutions. Let's consider how best to achieve that goal.

- Different generations need to communicate with each another about it, in collaborative, hands-on, deliberately multigenerational conversations. See The World Café model for a particularly effective way of holding productive and meaningful conversations among people with seemingly disparate perspectives.

- Generations need to explore alternative scenarios and solutions together based on the probable and the preferred future, not the past.

- Investigate generational partnerships, such as job sharing/mentorship arrangements, that enable two people to be employed instead of one, enable training costs and salary to combine, stretching a company's dollar and quickening the pace at which younger employees can gain the skills, knowledge, and some of the experience they need to be more valuable to that company and the marketplace.

- Encourage people over 60 to remain employed by starting their own businesses, whether less complex solopreneur home offices or larger operations that would remove the competition for the same job between two generations and also generate employment.

Businesses Focus: Helping Others Strengthen Their Relationships

For all the new, timesaving technology that's rolled out each year, we somehow seem to have less and less time available to us. Any business that brings extended families and communities together to help one another out and save time is bound to hit a ready market.

Business owners: How can you or your business save people time in ways that specifically allow them to have more meaningful time? With their children? Their parents? Volunteering themselves? What plot holes are there in the present story of your community? Where are the gaps that need attention? How can you fill them?

Employees planning your exit: Now is the time to research and develop preferred scenarios that could serve you, your colleagues, and your business, such as a consultant relationship or part-time substitute situation that enables everyone to take "meaning days," along with the traditional vacation time and sick time. To get the most out of your next phase of life and work, consider hiring a master certified career and business coach who truly understands the unique challenges and opportunities for those in the 40-plus range.

Business Focus:
The Changing Needs of Grandparents

When thinking about the needs of Baby Boomers and Matures, offering products and services for children may not even be on our radar. Yet grandparents and later-life parents are spending more time and money on children than ever before. There's visionary potential for businesses in focusing on ways to help grandparents spend more quality time strengthening their relationships with their grandchildren and children. If you are a grandparent who is also an entrepreneur (or in the planning stage of starting your own business), you have a prime opportunity to look at your own needs and desires, then align them with what others in your tribe are seeking.

Solopreneurs and large corporations alike need to recognize that the Baby Boomer market is essential to their bottom lines. Ageless Women are in a unique position—they have the opportunity to serve this market just as they are in this market to be served.

Growing (B)older

Vast numbers of innovators in midlife and beyond are working in companies, science, academia, and more. Studies show that the most successful companies are started by entrepreneurs over 55 years old. And you could join their ranks.

If you've ever felt that there's a bigger purpose inside you yet to be realized, then you would be selling yourself short by not uncovering that purpose. Don't make the mistake of thinking it's too late for you. Awakening the visionary voice inside can squelch your doubts and illuminate a vision you will be driven to pursue with passion and purpose toward profit.

Why do people postpone that first step towards a new future? We think too much! All too often, fearful thoughts rule, bringing us more things to fear, and this cycle perpetuates itself. Visionary thoughts do not produce change if we simply sit around thinking and waiting for change to appear. You couldn't have achieved any of your life's accomplishments without one thing—action.

For those going through life stage shifts, particularly at midlife and beyond, these greater societal shifts and story conflicts run parallel to the transitions and upheaval in our personal and professional lives. The chaos and uncertainty are coming from all sides, and it's tempting to hang on for dear life to anything stable and certain we can find, even if doing so means remaining in an unfulfilling career or toxic work environment.

Now is the time to create order from the chaos and build the aspirational Ageless future we want to live in and leave behind as a legacy for generations to come. That future hinges on recognizing the needs of the Boomer market. If you snooze, you lose! Now is the time to help your business join the small percentage of marketers who understand what is coming, leaping ahead to snatch up segments of this market.

Many of us let our visionary voice slumber because we're unsure of the actions we need to take, and we stumble on the idea that the first step must be a big one. But we need not begin with monumental change. The Butterfly Effect is alive and well—one small action, the flapping of a butterfly's wings, can cause a chain reaction of other small actions that build up into monumental events.

The results can be nothing short of world changing. The more of us who flap our wings, the bigger the effect we can have on our lives, the lives of our families and communities, and ultimately the planet. We can create an Ageless world. ❯

*Only those who see the invisible
can do the impossible.*

~ Karen Sands

GRAY IS THE NEW GREEN

Resources

You've Always Known You Were Meant for More

R eading about what is possible for you and for our world can spark your own realizations, discoveries, and BIG ideas. Don't let them slip away! **No matter your circumstances or your age or life stage, you can start acting now to fulfill your potential to transform your life, your work, and your world.**

And you don't have to go it alone. You will find books, card decks, and coaching services available for purchase, as well as numerous **FREE** tools for taking the next steps, at www.KarenSands.com. Check back regularly for ongoing information about the future and a continuous stream of new offerings. (You can also follow Karen on Twitter, LinkedIn, Facebook and Pinterest to get the latest updates.)

Here are just a fraction of the resources you will find at www.KarenSands.com today and in the near future:

- If you're 40-plus or serve the Boomer market, Karen's **Ageless Beat blog** offers a wealth of information, strategies, and guidance for you to make **the next** several decades your most visionary yet (at www. KarenSands.com/ageless-beat-blog).

- Download **FREE and low-cost e-books and mini print books**, such as *A Glimpse of Tomorrow's Future, The Greatness Challenge, Mastering Reinvention, An Ageless Story,* and *Crossing the Canyon*, at www.KarenSands. com/bookstore. Many more are in development.

- Also download **video and audio interviews, reports, how-tos**, and much more at www.KarenSands.com.

- Get your copy of *Visionaries Have Wrinkles* (print and e-book) which continues receiving rave reviews for conversations with women visionaries who share their no-holds-barred inspirational points of view on growing older boldly, wisely, and visibly to reshape the future of aging for all of us. Or download a pdf chapter to get acquainted with these visionaries. Make sure you check out the companion card deck, *Visionaries Have Wrinkles Reflections Card Deck*, and the companion workbook, *Visionaries Have Wrinkles Reflections Journal.* Available at www.KarenSands. com/bookstore and Amazon.

- Sign up for the **FREE monthly Ageless Beat newsletter** (www.KarenSands.com/ageless-beat-newsletter) to follow the latest conversations about how post-40 women and those who serve them can transform their lives, businesses, and the world.

- Browse **Ageless Experts** at www.KarenSands.com/ ageless-experts for articles by professionals who offer expert wisdom on various aspects of the future for and by women 40-plus (also the men in their lives) and for those who serve this market by offering services, products, and opportunities.

- Find out more about **FREE interactive forums, webinars, upcoming podcasts, workshops, and retreats**.

- **Expand the new language of our evolving Ageless Story by sharing words and phrases** you find or create as you make your way on your Ageless Quest. Send them to Karen@KarenSands.com for inclusion in our continuously expanding Glossary at www.KarenSands.com/glossary.

- Check back regularly for **new readings and links** at www.KarenSands.com/ageless-reads-links, or share your own recommendations at Karen@KarenSands.com.

- Find out about **coaching tailored to 40-plus women and men** for creating **sustainable Ageless businesses** and **full, meaningful Ageless lives** at www.KarenSands.com/ageless-coaching. Get one-to-one and group coaching, career, retirement, or semi-retirement planning to monetize what matters most to you and your clients. For details, contact Karen@KarenSands.com.

- Learn **how to stay in sync with the people who keep you in business,** especially those entering and moving through midlife and beyond. Read more at www.KarenSands.com/Media.

- Contact Karen about **corporate trainings and speaking,** especially on how to **leverage Boomer knowledge workers,** prepare for **post-50 futures,** and promote

intergenerational collaboration and innovation in the workplace. Read more at www.KarenSands.com/Media.

- You are invited to send **your stories and recommended readings** to Karen at Karen@KarenSands.com so she can share them with other readers on her site and her blog at www.KarenSands.com/ageless-beat-blog. ❯❯

About Karen Sands

Karen Sands has spent decades transforming conversations about Positive Aging, women, and the future, culminating in paving a more vibrant age-friendly way forward for age 40-plus women in the twenty-first century. In ushering in *The Ageless Way*, Sands capitalizes on tomorrow's trends today to illuminate a new story, a narrative fostering a life of unlimited meaning, satisfaction, impact and legacy-making, as well as money-making futures that matter. Karen shakes up perceptions that are limiting and outdated, transforming them into new possibilities that turn aging and ageism upside down. Her work aims to catapult women to the forefront of the business of aging as innovative social entrepreneurs, change-makers, visionary leaders, and discerning high-value consumers. Karen brings together the best practices of sustainable business and avant-garde approaches to timeless living and unlimited Ageless Aging. In doing so, she prepares us to rock our age by generating and utilizing innovative, intergenerational gero-businesses and services partnered with civic engagement. She is a "Visionary with Wrinkles," a CCE-BCC and ICF-MCC certified Master and Mentor Coach, a TED support Master Coach, the leading Educational GeroFuturist on the Longevity Economy, and author/creator of *Visionaries Have Wrinkles*, *Gray is the New Green,* as well as *The Ageless Way* book, services, and program. Sands is also an online entrepreneur, speaker, publisher, and multi-book author/blogger. Karen Sands propels women and men across generations to usher in *The Ageless Way* and radically reinvent the true meaning of growing older at any age—in life and in business."

Want more of *The Ageless Way*?
GET THE COMPLETE BOOK
at <u>www.KarenSands.com</u>